FILLED

with

HIS LOVE

Strengthening Our Attachment to *God* and to *Others*

Russell T. Osguthorpe

D1604055

CFI

An imprint of Cedar Fort, Inc.
Springville, Utah

WHAT OTHERS ARE SAYING ABOUT
FILLED WITH HIS LOVE

Instructive and edifying. Russell Osguthorpe, a true disciple-scholar, helps readers strengthen even their most difficult relationships with God, family, friends, others, and themselves. *Filled with His Love: Strengthening Our Attachment to God and to Others* includes useful applications of the doctrines and practices of the restored gospel of Jesus Christ and the principles of truth found in social science research. An important book written for the difficult days in which we live.

—DANIEL K JUDD, former dean of Religious Education, Brigham Young University

We all desire to feel loved and to love others, but most of us question if we are truly capable of healthy relationships. This book is essential in understanding the core of relational attachments and strengthening our bond with others and God to experience more inflowing and outflowing of love.

—JULIE HERNANDO, founder of Lighthouse Sanctuary, the Philippines

Filled with His Love teaches the two great commandments through stories and principles that enable the least of us to participate in God's work to bless His children. Russell Osguthorpe shares how attaching ourselves to God will empower us to attach ourselves with God's children and ultimately attach His children with Him, uniting all involved and erasing all lines between being a good friend, parent, missionary, minister, and Christian.

—TIMOTHY OVERTON, Esq. and diversity, equity and inclusion consultant for Belonging, LLC

Secure attachment is love. Love is the antidote. Love is the solution. God's love for us. And our love for God and all His children, including ourselves. This is the simple yet profound message of Russell Osguthorpe's latest book, *Filled with His Love: Strengthening Our Attachment to God and to Others*. Love is the animating power that makes enduring, meaningful, nurturing, and saving attachment possible. As a master storyteller and teacher, Osguthorpe leads readers through a page-turner of profundity and insight while remaining engagingly accessible. Brilliant and beautiful, Osguthorpe's book is filled with stories and gentle wisdom that are inspiring and instructive, reinforcing the power of love to securely attach us to what matters most: God, others, and ourselves. Reading this book by my mentor was a privilege, a treasure, a gift—all from the man who has shown me and so many others so much love.

—TAYLOR HALVORSON, best-selling author and speaker, associate teaching professor of entrepreneurship, Marriott School of Management, Brigham Young University

I could hardly put down *Filled with His Love: Strengthening our Attachments to God and to Others*. Russell Osguthorpe shares deep gospel insights and brings them to life with scriptural examples and his own culturally diverse experiences in locations like Tahiti, China, and Africa and from the prison to the temple. I kept reading to see what amazing event came next and what I would learn about attachments. I grew to love the people in his life: Amanda—the child adopted from a dismal and uncaring orphanage; Malu—the thirteen-year-old girl brutally separated from her mom in war; the sweet couple taking the sacrament in Tahiti; Grandma Bessie; the man imprisoned for life; Russell's sweet wife; his father, Wes; his true friend, Skip; and so many others. Pondering this book greatly enhanced how I view my attachments to God and others.

—JANE HANSEN LASSETER, dean of the College of Nursing, Brigham Young University

For my parents, Wes and Iva,
who taught me the meaning of
safe, secure, enduring attachment
by the way they lived their lives.

NOTE: The author will donate all royalties from the sale of this book to charitable organizations that serve children and families who struggle with attachment disorder.

© 2022 Russell T. Osguthorpe
All rights reserved.

No part of this book may be reproduced in any form whatsoever, whether by graphic, visual, electronic, film, microfilm, tape recording, or any other means, without prior written permission of the publisher, except in the case of brief passages embodied in critical reviews and articles.

This is not an official publication of The Church of Jesus Christ of Latter-day Saints. The opinions and views expressed herein belong solely to the author and do not necessarily represent the opinions or views of Cedar Fort, Inc. Permission for the use of sources, graphics, and photos is also solely the responsibility of the author.

ISBN 13: 978-1-4621-4144-9

Published by CFI, an imprint of Cedar Fort, Inc.
2373 W. 700 S., Springville, UT, 84663
Distributed by Cedar Fort, Inc., www.cedarfort.com

Library of Congress Control Number: 2021950820

Cover design by Courtney Proby
Cover design © 2022 Cedar Fort, Inc.

Printed in the United States of America

10 9 8 7 6 5 4 3 2 1

Printed on acid-free paper

CONTENTS

ACKNOWLEDGMENTS

I want to thank those who helped me through each cycle of writing and revising this book. My wife, Lolly, listened to me read every word of each chapter and gave me support and suggestions as no one else could. She continues to teach me about the eternal importance of attachment every day. Since their birth, our children have helped us learn how sacred parent-child attachment really is. Without such learning this book would not have been possible. In addition, John Hilton III, David A. Whetten, and Sharon Black reviewed earlier versions of the book and offered valuable recommendations that not only improved the manuscript but spurred me on to complete it. I am blessed to have such friends.

FOREWORD

T he author of this book, Russell T. Osguthorpe, asserts that the very reason for earth life is to learn to love. He goes on to explain that every experience can teach us more about the power and force of love, especially the love of this earth's Creators, our own Heavenly Father and his beloved Son, whose mission is love.

If this is so, then the inspired ideas that the author prescribes to strengthen earthly and eternal attachments is a promising path that can benefit every aspect of our lives. I wrote the following a few decades ago.

LOVE CLOSES THE DISTANCE

Dear Lord,
Thank you,
You've helped us
See your world,
Touch it,
Hold it
In our hands
And stand
Humbled
By the grandness
Of it all.

You've pushed it
So close
That we could
Scarcely breathe
Without
Fogging the glasses
Of the man
Beside us.

You knew
That this familiarity
Would breed in us
A burgeoning
Love.

It is the same with You, Lord.
Love closes the distance
Between us.

The Author's Introduction explains, "This book is about how to recognize, develop, and increase our capacity to love as God loves until His love literally fills us." He quotes Joseph Smith, who said believing in the great love we receive from the Father and the Son was good doctrine,

> This is good doctrine. It tastes good. I can taste the principles of eternal life, and so can you. They are given to me by the revelations of Jesus Christ, and I know that when I tell you these words of eternal life as they are given to me, you taste them, and I know that you believe them. . . . You are bound to receive them as sweet, and rejoice more and more.

This metaphor reminds us of the scripture in Alma 32:42 which describes the fruit of faith. "By and by ye shall pluck the fruit thereof, which is most precious, which is sweet above all that is sweet and which is white above all that is white, yea, and pure above all that is pure; and ye shall feast upon this fruit even until ye are filled, that ye hunger not neither shall you thirst."

See also Moroni 7:48, "Pray unto the Father with all the energy of heart, that ye may be filled with this love, which He hath bestowed upon all who are true followers of his Son, Jesus Christ . . . that when he shall appear, we shall be like him, for we shall see him as he is."

The author also refers to Elder Neal A. Maxwell's assertion, which uses the same metaphor and suggests agency is the key to developing our taste for truth, "We are also to use our agency so that we come to prefer, and even strongly desire, the taste of gospel goodness, sweetness, and joy. Only those who have significantly developed the taste buds of the soul will be partially prepared for the incredible beauties of the world ahead."

The last section of the book, Part 3, discusses how we can strengthen our attachments. It is an inspiring "To Do" list, an example of which follows:

Under the heading, *Growing in Holiness,* the author describes his own encounter with a brightening light filtering through the window of the Temple. As he describes his new understanding of how one can "grow in Holiness," the reader can catch a glimpse of the hope for his own enlightenment. As I read the following passage, I could see myself in the temple experiencing the same spiritual yearnings as the author: "Still seated in that room with light flooding in, I pray silently with all the spiritual energy I possess, that I can be filled with His love for me and that I can show that love more genuinely, more graciously, more freely to others, so that holiness can increase in me, that it may continue to enlarge my view so that one day I can see Him as He is."

This book allows one to feel, as the author explains that "love always needs to flow in both directions—from one person to another and back again, from us to God and back from God to us." The image reminded me of a cherished verse in the *New Testament:* "We love Him because He first loved us." To say I recommend this book is an understatement. It has powerfully enriched my understanding of the love of and for the Lord. And even more so, His unfailing love for me. And so it is.

—ANN MADSEN

INTRODUCTION

Of all the problems we face in mortality, the most vexing is not the lack of money or even the lack of food and water. It is the lack of love—the inability to receive and give love as the Savior did. If our physical body receives the necessary nourishment but our spirit does not receive and give love, our time on earth has no meaning. We may as well not exist.

One of the strongest, most penetrating statements in all of scripture appears in Mormon's final witness about the importance of charity: "For if ye have not charity, ye are nothing" (Moroni 7:46). This is a powerful assertion: whatever qualities we might possess—fame, money, or talent—we are still nothing unless we possess the love of Christ.

Without this love we are not merely diminished. We are not merely less than we could be. We are simply nothing at all. We are not a fully living, breathing human being. We are like a cup with no water, a book with no words, a heart without motion. Lacking this love, we are like those mentioned in the introduction of the Book of Mormon: feeling that they have been forgotten and "cast off forever."

This book is about how to recognize, develop, and increase our capacity to love as God loves until His love literally fills us. Like the cup that is filled one drop at a time until it overflows; the book that fills us one word, one phrase, one story at a time until it inspires and lifts; the heart that gains strength and rhythm so perfectly that it heals and strengthens the heart of another.

Few would argue that any human on the planet has enough love, or that anyone has developed the capacity to give all the love that is needed. In her book *The Simple Path*, Mother Teresa has expressed the need for an increase of love: "The greatest disease in the West today is not TB or leprosy; it is being unwanted, unloved, and uncared for. We can cure physical diseases with medicine, but the only cure for loneliness, despair, and hopelessness is love. There are many in the world who are dying for a piece of bread but there are many more dying for a little love. The poverty in the West is a different kind of poverty—it is not only a poverty of loneliness but also of spirituality. There's a hunger for love, as there is a hunger for God."[1]

Our relationships with others are ultimately based on our relationship with God. This is why loneliness requires His help. If we do not reach up to God, we will not reach out to others. In essence, we will not know how to love His children if we do not know how to love Him. The closer we draw to God, the closer we will draw to others, and the closer we draw to others, the more the scourge of loneliness will be transformed by the miracles of friendship, inclusion, and oneness.

When I began thinking about this book, the subtitle that came to mind was "Strengthening Relationships with God and with Others." Then I started to consider the word *attachments* as an alternative to *relationships*. The more I thought about this word, the more I liked it. When someone is attached to another, the person is full of fondness and affection for the other. One might say, full of love—not just any kind of love but a love that is fueled by devotion, closeness, mutual trust, and fidelity—the love that God has for us.

---

1. Mother Teresa, *A Simple Path* (New York: Ballantine Books, 2007), 79.

I don't want simply to have a relationship with God; I want to be attached to Him, devoted to Him, close to Him, and true to Him. After all, He is devoted to me, close to me, and true to me. This kind of association extends to my family members and close friends. I'm related to my family members by shared genes, but I want our bond to be more than genetic. I want to be emotionally and spiritually *attached* to them.

The words *attached* or *attachment* do not appear in the scriptures with the notable exception of one entry in the Bible Dictionary under the word *sheep*: "Shepherds still, as of old, go before the sheep, and the sheep follow, being apparently more or less *attached* to their masters, whose voice they instantly recognize" (emphasis added).

Sheep are often likened to us, and Christ to the shepherd. In the Bible Dictionary, this attachment is centered on devotion. The degree to which we are devoted to the Savior determines how readily we recognize and respond to His voice, His example, and His teachings. The relationship we have with God the Father and His Son, Jesus Christ, is an attachment relationship. It is a relationship characterized not only by fondness but by a deep, abiding love. This love is the first and most important commandment we have been given: "Thou shalt love the Lord thy God with all thy heart, with all thy might, mind, and strength" (D&C 59:5). Our attachment to God is stronger, deeper, and closer than any other relationship we forge in mortality. And the second commandment is like the first: "Thou shalt love thy neighbor as thyself" (D&C 59:6).

The way we relate to money, food, or politics may be necessary aspects of mortality. But when we approach the end of life on earth, all we care about is how we relate to God and His children. I worked for decades with a man who was intellectually gifted. His ability to instruct and inspire with his words was impressive. But at times our relationship was strained due to the pressures of the workplace. Then, at an age when most might be contemplating retirement, he became gravely ill, requiring hospitalization for months. During that time, I visited him periodically, even when he was in intensive care. He was connected to tubes and masks and machines without which he would not have been able to breathe. On one occasion, shortly after I entered his hospital room, he looked up at me from his bed, briefly removed his oxygen mask, and with great effort said, "I love you, Russ."

My friend knew that he did not have long to live, and all that mattered to him during those final months was to make certain that those who had been close to him knew that he loved them. I am certain also that his concern for others grew out of his love for God. He was at his core a spiritual man. On that day in the hospital, he helped me see more clearly the centrality of relationships to our existence as humans. So a question arises: If our attachment to God and with others are the most important aspects of mortal life, how can we learn to love and be loved more fully, more completely? This book is an attempt at answering that question.

This book contains three parts. In part one, I introduce the idea of attachment and describe how parent-child relationships can eventually affect adult relationships (particularly marriage) in either positive or negative ways. In part two, I discuss the centrality of one's attachment to God and how our attachment to God affects all other relationships. Finally, in part three, I focus on how we can strengthen our attachment to God and to others. This final section of the book rests on the assumption that strengthening our attachment to God and to others is, in fact, the primary purpose of mortality. My hope is that the suggestions offered in part three can help readers examine their own relationships and put into practice those suggestions that will lead to stronger, healthier attachments with those they love.

Part One

ATTACHMENT AND LOVE

I begin this section by describing my own search for answers regarding human relationships. It has not been a seamless, step-by-step systematic search, but rather a start-and-stop, hit-and-miss, here-a-little, there-a-little quest. In recent years I have focused more on the idea of attachment and what it means to form a deep, lasting, loving relationship with another. Because those who have studied the principles of attachment began their own search by observing the parent-child attachment, I will also begin there.

An infant enters the world completely dependent on others. The attachment that develops between the infant and the care-giver—most often the parent—is a sacred bond that gives life not only to the infant but also to the parent. Holding a newborn in your arms is like holding eternity. Nothing quite compares to it in mortality, and no one can explain the depth and breadth of the feelings that a newborn brings to eager parents whose capacity to love is beginning to increase in a new and miraculous way.

Prophets and apostles have always tried to help parents understand the profound blessings that await them as they welcome a new child into their home.[1] They make it clear that the child is a gift from the Lord, that both parents have a key role in the development of the child, and that both can be attached to the child forever.[2] The quality of the parent-child attachment is the key. A relationship is never simply good or bad. Rather, every relationship is unique because each person is unique. Therefore, a parent can't discover a formula that will work the same with every child. Each parent-child attachment must be formed anew.

1. Neil L. Andersen, "Children," *Ensign*, October 2011.
2. The First Presidency and Quorum of the Twelve Apostles, "The Family: A Proclamation to the World" (Salt Lake City, Utah: The Church of Jesus Christ of Latter-day Saints, 1995), q=proclamation+on+the+family&rlz=1C9BKJA_enUS865US865&oq=proclamation&aqs=chrome.1.69i 57j0l3.4721j0j4&hl=en-US&sourceid=chrome-mobile&ie=UTF-8

When a secure, healthy attachment is formed between a parent and a child, the attachment has two primary qualities: It offers the child a safe haven and a secure base. A safe haven means that the child can turn to the parent and seek refuge in time of distress. The child feels safe in the presence of either parent. A secure base is present when attachment with parents provides the child confidence to explore the world, to learn, and to discover. One parent may be more adept at offering the child a safe haven, while the other may find it easier to provide a secure base. This may be one reason that prophets have taught in "The Family: A Proclamation to the World" that whenever possible children should be reared by both a father and a mother.

What happens if children do not form a healthy, strong attachment to their parents—if they don't experience the safe haven or the secure base? In what ways does the attachment experienced by a child in the early years affect relationships as the child matures? Or do most children simply outgrow the problems of unhealthy attachments? These are questions worth pondering, not only for parents but for anyone who wants to gain a deeper understanding of the origins of their own relationship style. Equally important is the question about how parent-child relationships might affect one's ability to form healthy attachments later in life, especially the marriage relationship. Because our concept of the new and everlasting covenant of marriage is so central to our doctrine, I will explore how principles of attachment can help us as we seek an eternal mate and, once we find that person, build a joyful, life-giving bond with them.

MY JOURNEY

I will not leave you comfortless:
I will come to you.

—John 14:18

I'm not certain what prompted my need to understand how people form relationships, but it has always puzzled me. Why are some people so easy to get along with, while others are so difficult? Why do some marriages succeed, while others fail? These and similar questions perplexed me. One thing I came to understand is that perplexity is like the match that lights the flame of learning. Without the match (without perplexity), no real learning occurs. Asking a question to solve the perplexity is like striking the match, but at the beginning of this particular journey I could not even form the question. I could just feel an unsettling sense of discomfort.

My earliest memory of this quandary began on the way home from my summer job when I was fifteen years old. I had just obtained my driver's license and had purchased a used car, so I was the go-to friend when someone needed a ride. Shawn, an acquaintance at work, asked if I could give him a ride home that day. I agreed. Even though we did not know each other very well, on the way home he began to divulge how frustrated he was with life, that he was planning to quit his job, leave his parents' home, and move in with another family member. Then, in a voice without any emotion, he said, "And I'm thinking of leaving the Church. I just don't think I believe in God anymore."

I had to hold a little tighter to the steering wheel so I could keep the car on the road. I had never known anyone who had chosen to leave the Church or even someone who did not believe in God. I kept driving, but I felt like we needed to stop and talk more about his plans. I had a strong urge to convince him to rethink everything, but he was determined and I could tell my urging would not make any difference. He had made up his mind. I dropped him off at his home and never saw him again. He quit work, moved out of his parents' home, and left the Church. After I dropped him off I kept thinking about how different Shawn was from me. I could never think of cutting ties with my parents or the Church, and certainly not God. I was puzzled at how he came to such a troubling juncture in his life. I was perplexed, but I couldn't strike the match yet because I wasn't sure how to ask the question.

A few years later I was called to serve in the French Polynesian Mission, where I served with nine companions in the first six months in Tahiti. As soon as I began to adjust to one companion, I was transferred and assigned a new companion. I found that forming a healthy, effective companionship did not happen automatically. I served under two mission presidents, each of whom had profound influence on me during my mission and throughout my life, and their wives had as much positive impact on me as did they. Forming these relationships with companions, my mission presidents, and their wives became central to my happiness as a missionary. My world was broadening. I could no longer associate only with my family members and friends of my own choosing as I had done back home. Not only did I need to meet new people, as we did while tracting, but I was required as well to form meaningful relationships with those I taught and with whom I served. Questions began to emerge in my mind about how best to form good relationships—not that I asked such questions systematically at that early stage in my life, but the questions were always there in the background. So the perplexity was becoming a bit more focused.

Following my mission I found my eternal companion. There was no perplexity there. Ours was a courtship without the ups and downs that many experience. We knew quite soon after we began dating that we would marry. I remember one occasion after only a few weeks of marriage that helped define our relationship. I was sitting in the kitchen of our one-bedroom apartment, reading a textbook for one of my courses when my wife came through the door. I greeted her as always, but her response gave me pause. "Is there something wrong?" I asked. Responding almost too quickly and too confidently, she said, "No, nothing's wrong!" Sensing that she wasn't telling me the whole story, I asked again, "Are you okay?" She again seemed to respond a little too sharply, "Nothing's wrong!" The words seemed right, but I could sense that something was actually wrong and she didn't want to talk about it.

I invited her to sit with me at the table where I was studying. Then I implored, "I think I must have done something, and I actually need to know what I did so I can fix it." After a long pause, she divulged what I had done earlier in the day that had hurt her feelings. I apologized, and then the conversation became even more interesting. She explained how her parents, when they were at odds with each other, would not communicate with each other for a few days. Her mother would bake her famous apple pie, and then her father would know he had been forgiven. No discussion, just a peace offering. I suggested that this was not the way I wanted to relate to her as my wife. I wanted to know how she was feeling, even if those feelings were negative and especially if I was the cause of her frustrations. We both agreed, and that short interaction helped develop a pattern for communication that strengthened our relationship throughout our marriage.

Earlier experiences with my friendships and then companionships formed on my mission led me to ask more questions about relationships, but marriage brought a whole new dimension to my search for answers. Marriage was qualitatively different. My wife and I were together not only in mortality but for eternity. As our relationship matured, I noticed that if we had disagreed on something, which we did from time to time, or even if I sensed that we were not seeing something in the same way, even a small thing, I could not be productive at work. I learned that I could not walk out the door until we had talked through a problem we needed to resolve. My feelings were the same ones I felt during the earlier conversation at that small kitchen table in our first apartment. My perplexity was about relationships, and my specific questions at that particular moment all centered around marriage. It wasn't a question of how could we get along with each other; it was a question of how could we bring real joy to each other every day forever?

When children were born, my desire to help them know how to give and receive love became as important for me as was my marriage. As parents, we wanted to make certain that love flowed in every direction in our family—parent-to-child love, sibling-to-sibling love, and from each one of us in the family to extended family members and friends. Questions kept coming about how to help children love and be loved. When our children began to argue and "fight and quarrel one with another" (Mosiah 4:14), we would have them take a time-out and sit in the designated "mad chair" until they could control their emotions, forgive their sibling, and give each other a heartfelt hug. We found that helping children form healthy relationships was our top family priority.

As time went on, church callings I received caused me to continue to ask questions about relationships. How could I gain the trust of the fourteen-year-old young men in my teachers quorum? How could those I was ministering to know that I actually cared about them? Those were important questions, but I soon found that I did not need to worry only about how I was relating to others but how the ones I had been called to serve were relating to one another. As an elders quorum president, I became very concerned in one meeting when two members of the quorum began arguing over a doctrinal point in the lesson. As the argument grew more heated, I felt compelled to assume control of the meeting momentarily and share a verse of scripture that explained clearly that we should not have contention over points of doctrine (see D&C 10:63). My own perplexity about relationships was expanding to include questions about how I could help others with their relationship problems.

When I was called to serve as a stake president of a married students stake, my questions continued to mount. My stake members were mostly newlyweds, and so many were confronting the challenges that married couples face as they adjust to each other. Even though most couples in the stake were navigating these adjustments successfully, a few couples were considering divorce. I asked the bishops in my stake to refer such couples to me whenever possible. Their experiences adjusting to marriage were not at all like my own. Oftentimes their courtships had been rocky, and their marriages even rockier. I urged them to get professional help from family therapists, but their bishop and I were their sources for ecclesiastical help.

At this point my desire to understand more about relationship counseling peaked. I was not a trained therapist, but I began to study all I could about such counseling and to have discussions with friends who were professionals. After my release as stake president, I continued to search for answers that could help explain the origin and possible cures for relationship problems. I wanted to be able to help those who came to me for help with their marriages. Eventually I began studying attachment theory, a theory that asserts that many of our relationship issues as adults can be traced back to the ways we related to our parents as young children. I recognized that this was only one way of explaining relationship problems, but I found it useful in my efforts to help those who came to me for help. My questions had finally led me to something I could use to help others understand their own challenges and begin to deal with them. However, I soon found that this was only the beginning of my initial perplexity with relationships. This is what I had learned thus far:

- Welcome perplexity.
- Don't force questions. Let them emerge on their own.
- Remain open even to the smallest particle of an answer.
- Let those you serve prompt your search.
- Listen to others while staying close to the Spirit.

We often speak of "experiential learning," and in the end, this is the way we learn our most important lessons. Some of our experience is direct, and some is vicarious. We often see through another's eyes and come to understand their experience, which changes the way we view ourselves and others. Focusing on our relationships leads us closer to God and each other. In the next chapter, I talk about the concept of attachment and how it contributes so fundamentally to our joys and sorrows.

ATTACHMENT

*True autonomy relies on feeling securely
connected to other human beings.*[1]

—Nora Samaran

During the same decades that I was asking questions about relationships in my own life, a team of psychiatrists and psychologists in England were asking questions about how young children relate to their parents. I was attracted to their research because it focused not on emotional health in general but on only one thing: relationships. And because that was my question, I was drawn to their writings.

As these researchers observed young children in a nursery school environment, they noticed the differences in each child's reaction as their parents brought them into the classroom and then later in the day how the children reacted when their parents came to retrieve them. Some children could almost not bear to be separated from their mothers at the beginning of the day, while other children immediately began playing with the others, barely noticing that their mothers had left the room. At the end of the day, when the mothers returned, some children could not run fast enough to be gathered into their mother's arms, while others

---

1.   Nora Samaran, *Turn the World Upside Down: The Emergence of a Nurturance Culture* (Chico, CA: AK Press, 2019), 86.

wanted to keep playing, and still others did not want to get close to their mothers.

Those observing the children gradually settled on words that best described the differences in how children related to their mothers. Children who felt comfortable immediately interacting with other children and caregivers were said to have a secure attachment. These children felt comfortable even if there were strangers present and felt confident to engage with others even if their mother were not present. Children who became inconsolable at the departure of their mother and had difficulty interacting with others were said to have an anxious attachment. Finally, those who seemed to have no interest in being with their mother were said to have an avoidant attachment. I have greatly oversimplified the theory for purposes of this book, so if you want to explore more about how attachment theory developed, feel free to check the references I've included at the end of this book (e.g., *Attachment Theory and Religion* by Cherniak, et al.).

The value I saw in those who studied attachment was that it gave me a new and better way of talking about and thinking about relationships. An attachment is a close, affectionate bond between two people, such as the bond that forms naturally between a mother or a father and their child. When the attachment is secure, children feel safe in the presence of their parent because the home is a safe place where the child does not need to fear separation. They know that if the parent leaves, the parent will return and that they will be loved by the parent. These children also have confidence to explore the world around them because the parents have provided them with a secure base by encouraging them to search, explore, and learn from their surroundings. The importance of all of these findings is that when young children experience healthy secure attachments, they are more likely to be able to form healthy secure attachments as adults. Likewise, when young children develop unhealthy anxious or avoidant attachments, they are more likely to approach adult relationships in unhealthy anxious or avoidant ways. In the words of Bruce D. Perry, who has studied childhood trauma, "Dismissive caregiving can lead to an unquenchable thirst for love. You cannot love if you have not been loved."[2]

Those who have served in their ward nursery or Primary organization can readily identify children with healthy secure attachment and those with unhealthy insecure attachment. Although all children develop some separation anxiety by their ninth month, most begin to deal with separation from a parent effectively by age two. Most of the children who do have an anxious or avoidant attachment pattern in their behavior usually have mild forms of the disorder, but to illustrate the consequences of severe attachment disorder, I share an experience I had while serving in the temple.

A temple is a quiet place, a place where adults and youth come to experience more closeness to God. But when parents come to be sealed to their children, the quiet is sometimes replaced with the echoes of a young child crying and even screaming. Temple workers scurry around trying to help, but the child often holds sway and stops only when volition conquers emotion. An extreme example of such a scene occurred when a family entered the temple to be sealed to Amanda.

Amanda was placed in an orphanage in Eastern Europe as an infant. In those early years she spent nearly all of her time in a cage-like crib that she could not escape. Her meals were delivered into the crib, but sometimes meals did not come when she was hungry, so she kept crying for food but to no avail. The children in the cribs surrounding her were crying just as Amanda, but no one came to comfort them. No one came to take away Amanda's fear. No one came to nourish her or hold her no matter how desperate her need. She was alone all day long with brief deliveries from people who seemed to have no voice, only food.

---

2. Bruce D. Perry and Oprah Winfrey, *What Happened to You?: Conversations on Trauma, Resilience, and Healing.* (New York: Flatiron Books, 2021).

Year after year Amanda remained confined in that over-crowded orphanage where no one seemed to know her or care for her. Because she heard so little speech, she failed to acquire language at the appropriate age. She had difficulty relating to other children or adults because they related so little to her. Physically weak and only half her normal size, she wanted only to retreat—to withdraw from the emptiness that engulfed her from morning until night.

Then one day a man and a woman were escorted to the room where she was lying on her bed trying to take a nap. She was frightened when she saw them—everything new frightened Amanda. The attendant explained that the visitors wanted to spend some time getting to know her. She was still frightened. No one ever wanted to "get to know her." "What does this mean?" she wondered. The couple tried not to be too eager, but two days before they had surveyed the children in the orphanage one after another and felt something special about Amanda. The wife turned to her husband and whispered, "I think we need to adopt this girl." They held each other for a moment, continuing to look at Amanda without her noticing.

Her husband smiled in agreement. They already had four of their own children, and they were not wealthy or looking for additional tasks to keep themselves busy. But they felt compelled to adopt Amanda, as if it were a call from heaven. They began the lengthy process of adoption, most of which took place after they had returned to their home in the United States. When the approvals were finally obtained, they made one more transatlantic trip to retrieve Amanda. She was still frightened when she saw them she and began crying incessantly—unlike any thirteen-year-old they had ever encountered.

The attendant explained that she would eventually stop crying but that she would need to self-soothe, as most other children had to do in the orphanage. They had never heard the term "self-soothe" before but soon discovered the disturbing meaning of the term in Amanda's case. Children who are raised in an orphanage seldom get the attention they need when they are in distress, so they just keep crying until they can soothe themselves since no one else is available to soothe them. For psychologically healthy people, self-soothing can be an effective strategy to regulate emotion, but for Amanda, it was the only strategy, because there was no one else to make her feel safe and cared for.

The flight back to the U.S. was grueling. Amanda had, of course, never flown before and was terrified most of the flight. The only relief from the crying came when they slipped a sedative into her drink. Once home, Amanda became acquainted with her new siblings—again an ordeal for everyone, but there were glimpses of hope during these early days that gave reassurance to the couple that the adoption was the right choice for them. As time passed, they knew they wanted to have Amanda sealed to them, so they called the temple and made the necessary arrangements.

Entering the temple was not an easy thing for Amanda, but by this time the family knew how to handle things. She was screaming when the family entered the temple and kept screaming for what seemed to be a very long time. As they entered a room in the temple where Amanda could be comforted, the mother had her sit on a chair and then left the room and let her cry. The mother explained, "Amanda was raised in an orphanage and never knew her birth parents. It might take ten or fifteen minutes, but she will eventually self-soothe and stop her crying." Although it seemed longer than fifteen minutes, Amanda finally stopped, just as her mother had said, and the sealing was performed.

Amanda can teach us much about attachment. As an infant and then a young child, she had no attachment to any adult. The caregivers at the orphanage were periodically present in her life but not permanently attached to her. They came and went like minutes ticking on a clock. She could never count on them, trust them, or feel genuine love from them. They had their own attachments to spouses or friends, but Amanda was not one of them. She was deprived of the most essential necessity of human life: love. Lack of nourishment had stunted her physical growth. That result was apparent to anyone who met Amanda for the first time. But what were the effects of love deprivation on Amanda?

Those who study attachment disorder would readily recognize the damage that had been done to Amanda in that orphanage. Her upbringing had made it disturbingly difficult for her to relate to other people. She had, in essence, been robbed of the usual developmental traits of trust, empathy, and other sensibilities that drew her to other people and helped her feel their love for her. When a child does not experience consistent, genuine love, the child often develops what has been called attachment disorder. When such a disorder is severe, as was Amanda's, it is called Reactive Attachment Disorder (RAD). RAD is perhaps the most extreme result of love deprivation—extreme but far too common. Researchers estimate that there are 153 million children worldwide living in orphanages and that those raised in such environments are five times as likely to develop RAD.

The following chart shows the different kinds of attachments that can form between a parent and a child. The attachment (or lack of attachment) that Amanda experienced is illustrated in the lower right quadrant: "Dysfunctional."

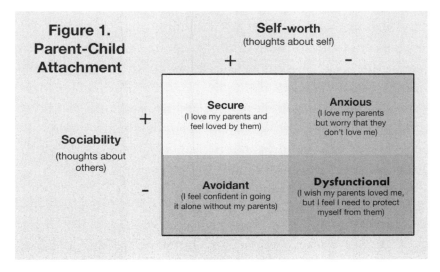

Figure 1. Parent-Child Attachment

Self-worth (thoughts about self)

+   −

Sociability (thoughts about others)

+

Secure (I love my parents and feel loved by them)

Anxious (I love my parents but worry that they don't love me)

−

Avoidant (I feel confident in going it alone without my parents)

Dysfunctional (I wish my parents loved me, but I feel I need to protect myself from them)

During her early childhood Amanda developed negative feelings toward others, as well as negative feelings toward herself. The more caregivers ignored or abused her, the more fearful she became that they would never return to help her. When they did come, she gradually learned (even subconsciously) that the safest approach was to avoid them because she did not want to be hurt by them. This is the most extreme of all attachment styles and by definition the most debilitating. Children with this type of dysfunctional attachment style are unable to form healthy relationships with others and will require therapy to overcome their disorder.

Children in the upper right quadrant, "Anxious," want to connect to their parents but are afraid that their parents will not reciprocate their love. Those in the lower left quadrant, "Avoidant," feel positive about themselves, so positive that they feel no need to rely on parental love. But even these positive feelings about oneself often arise from the insecurities they feel toward their parents. Those in the upper left quadrant, "Secure," eagerly love their parents and feel loved by them. Amanda clearly began her life in a negative environment that led to her inability to form healthy attachments, but following her adoption, she began the journey from fear and avoidance to safety, security, and enduring love.

When Mother Teresa asserted that the greatest disease in the West was "being unwanted, unloved, and uncared for," she was not referring only to those in orphanages, since orphanages are rare in the West. She was talking about children being ignored and neglected. Neglect can occur anywhere. Amanda's story illustrates the damage that neglect and mistreatment can do to a child. Some parents—even well meaning parents—might be neglectful of their children, not necessarily because they want to but because of their own inability to care for their children.

Amanda can teach us much about the dangers of love deprivation, not only for its effects on children but for the challenges that await such children as they mature. Everyone needs to experience secure attachment in life, and when such attachment does not occur early, it becomes more difficult to develop such attachment later in life. No one has too much love, the healthy life-giving love I am speaking of. While Amanda's story depicts a case of extreme love deprivation, too many do not experience healthy attachment in their childhood and youth. Some estimate that at least 50 percent of all adults suffer to some degree from Adult Attachment Disorder. This means that they have difficulty forming lasting close relationships as adults because they may lack empathy, distrust others, have difficulty processing positive emotions, are too rigid and controlling, or can be too impulsive.[3] Everyone could benefit from a clearer understanding of the principles of attachment and how those principles relate to the gospel of Jesus Christ and its emphasis on marriage and family relationships.

In summary:

The quality of childhood attachments can affect the quality of adult attachments.
Love is essential to life, as essential as are air and water.
Love deprivation can lead to serious emotional problems.
Safe, secure attachment brings peace and strength to both parent and child.

---

3. Michael Puskar, "The Prevalence of Attachment Disorder in Adults," *Better Help,* 2020, https://www.betterhelp.com/advice/personality-disorders/the-prevalence-of-attachment-disorder-in-adults/

MARRIAGE

Thou shalt love thy wife with all thy heart,
and shalt cleave unto her and none else.

—D&C 42:22

Because multiple studies have shown that the patterns of attachment a child develops are often similar to the patterns of attachment expressed in adulthood, the implications for the marriage relationship are clear.[1] One can easily see how forming a marriage relationship as an adult would be challenging for those who experience parental rejection early in life, as did Amanda. Marriage requires trust, openness, and security, qualities that Amanda did not enjoy as a child. Marriage is the only attachment that includes all forms of human intimacy. The only one that permits us to share our whole soul, body, and spirit with another. The only one that is meant to bring new life into the world. The only one that is founded on a covenant made with each other and with God. When we kneel at the altar in the temple and give ourselves to our spouse, we give everything: our innermost thoughts, our compete trust, and our total commitment. No other relationship is like it.

---

1. Amir Levine and Rachel S. E. Heller, *Attached: The New Science of Adult Attachment and How It Can Help You Find and Keep Love* (New York: Tarcher-Perigee, 2010).

A question that deserves to be asked by anyone who is married or who is contemplating marriage is this: How do my relationships with my family and friends affect the way I relate to my spouse? How does the attachment I have formed with God affect my marriage? We may not consciously think about it, but our attachments to parents, to others, and to God affect the kind of attachments we form in marriage.

The following diagram illustrates the types of attachments we might form in marriage—the degree to which we cleave to our spouse by describing how we see ourselves (self-worth) and how we see our spouse and others (sociability). The purpose of the diagram is to highlight characteristics of attachments to help illuminate the positive and negative styles of attachment in marriage.

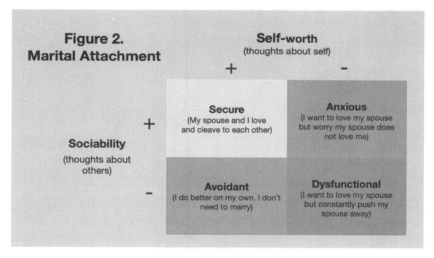

The goal in life is to establish long-lasting, joyful attachments, as seen in the upper left quadrant—marriages that are whole and healthy and in which each spouse creates a safe haven and secure base for the other and for their children. In this type of marriage the wife and husband cleave to each other in total fidelity. The wife and husband in this quadrant see themselves and each other as children of a loving Father in Heaven. They feel bound to God, close to Him, loved by Him. They have positive self-worth and positive approaches to others (sociability).

They are physically and spiritually intimate with each other and no one else. They trust each other completely, build each other, and lift each other closer to God.

The other three quadrants describe unhealthy marital attachments. In the upper right quadrant, individuals have positive thoughts about others but negative thoughts about themselves. They worry about their attachment to their spouse. They may see themselves as unworthy of love and also unworthy to have a healthy, lasting marriage. They worry that their spouse will see them the way they see themselves and will not be able to give them the love they wish they could receive—not because their spouse cannot love them but because they are not deserving of such love. They are in constant fear that they will be abandoned, because they may have been abandoned before, even early in their life.

In the lower right quadrant anxiety and fear also dominate the attachment, but in this case individuals feel they need to protect themselves because they cannot trust their spouse. They have been neglected or abused before, and they cannot bear to experience that hurt again. They avoid close relationships of all kinds because of the fear that is in them, somewhat akin to those who suffer from post traumatic stress syndrome. Those who have this dysfunctional attachment style actually seek relationships because they think that others can compensate for their inadequacies, but they have negative views of others and fear they will be hurt by others if they try to let them into their lives. These are adults who suffer from attachment disorder, the serious intersection between avoidant and anxious approaches to relationships.

Those in the lower left quadrant have an avoidant style of relating to others. Individuals with this style are extremely self-confident in their own right (or at least they seem on the outside to be confident), so confident that they do not feel that they need others. In their early life they found it more effective to remain at a distance, because close relationships only made life more difficult, more complex for them. As long as they could make their own decisions without interference from others, they felt more in control, so they dismissed others as intruders into their self-defined life.

I describe these attachment styles with broad brushstrokes simply to depict the vast array—actually infinitely vast array—of how people express and receive love. People do not fit neatly into boxes. Attachment styles blur together for every person. But the categories can help us see in ourselves and in others certain nuances in the very personal ways we relate to each other. The main reason for describing these styles is to aid looking intro-spectively at the way we relate to others as affected by the ways we related to our parents, siblings, and God as we grew to adulthood.

If a married couple both have secure attachment styles, the probability of forming a happy, healthy marriage is enhanced. However, if two people who marry both have an anxious or avoidant style, the marriage attachment will be more difficult to establish. The good news is that a recent study of more than 11,000 couples has shown that couples can overcome attachment deficiencies they may bring to the marriage if both spouses are committed to creating a secure marriage relationship.[2] Patterns of attachment developed early in life can be changed later in life.

While I was serving as a stake president, a couple came to me for help with their relationship. They had been married for about five years and had decided that they simply could not endure each other any longer. They said that they did not love each other any-more and were considering divorce. During our time together, they verbally picked at each other, chronicling every complaint that came to mind.

They shared some frustrations with each other that they had never shared before. I was surprised that they did not seem to know each other very well even though they had been married for

---

2. Douglas LaBier, "A Relationship Secret of the Happiest Couples: New Research," *Psychology Today*, August 19, 2020.

five years. Their words were harsh, laced with negative emotion and bitterness. The scene was not pleasant, either for them or for me. If I were to suggest their attachment styles, I would say that they were both primarily avoidant. They were quite sure of themselves separately and did not feel a real need to be together. This pattern shared by the two of them was one reason, I believe, they knew so little about each other's deepest desires. With the image of this discordant couple in your mind, let us recall the Savior's intercessory prayer in John 17.

The husband and wife I was counseling were obviously not at one in their marriage. They certainly were not cleaving to one another. They seemed distant even while sitting next to each other in front of me. And they were not at one with God. The Savior knew that becoming one would be our main challenge in mortality, and so this was His central plea: "I in them, and thou in me, that they may be made perfect (or complete) in one" (John 17:11). The word *one* appears in His prayer again and again. Then He revealed the way to become one—to truly cleave to each other. That is how to feel God's love. When we're at war with ourselves or with each other, as this couple was, we preclude ourselves from feeling the Lord's love, and when we do not feel loved by the Lord, our capacity to love others—especially our spouse—decreases dramatically.

The word *cleave* is particularly interesting because it has two meanings as a verb: (a) "to divide apart or separate" or (b) "to adhere or attach."[3] Few words have two meanings that are so directly opposite. But in the Old Testament, we read, "Thou didst cleave the earth with rivers" (Habbukuk 3:9), meaning rivers divided or separated one land from another. And yet the word is also used in the oft-quoted verse in the Old Testament: "Therefore shall a man leave his father and his mother, and shall cleave unto his wife: and they shall be one flesh" (Genesis 2:24; D&C 42:22; Abraham:18). This is an admonition for a husband

---

3. "Cleave 1 vt," *Oxford English Dictionary* (Oxford: Oxford University Press, 2004).

to adhere or attach himself to his wife and she to him—becoming one as the Savior prayed.

The instruction is not, of course, that we detach ourselves from our parents, that we forget them or ignore them. The attachment relationship that we had with our parents from birth has now been added upon, and we must cleave as strongly to our spouse as we once did as a newborn to our mother and father.

When the word *cleave* is used to mean attach, the scriptures admonish us to cleave to God, to our spouse, and to others. In the Book of Mormon, for example, the Lord urges us to "cleave unto charity" and to "cleave unto every good thing" (Moroni 7). When we attach ourselves to every good thing or to charity, we automatically attach ourselves to God's children—the recipients of our charity. When someone joins the Church, we welcome that person as a brother or a sister. We attach ourselves to our new member. Referring to the millennial day, Isaiah said, "For the Lord will have mercy on Jacob, and will yet choose Israel, and set them in their own land: and the strangers shall be joined with them, and they shall cleave to the house of Jacob" (Isaiah 14:1, 2 Nephi 24:1; Moses 3:24).

As fellow Saints we are asked to attach ourselves to one another as family members because we are literally the children of God. When new members move into the ward, we raise our hands to welcome them and agree to befriend them, to attach ourselves to them. Likewise, when a member is sustained to a new calling, the uplifted hand represents more than simple agreement with the call. The gesture signals a commitment to support the person as one friend supports another.

Jacob pleads with his people to "cleave unto God as he cleaveth unto you. And while his arm of mercy is extended towards you in the light of the day, harden not your hearts" (Jacob 6:5). Perhaps the most frequent use of the term *cleave* in the scriptures is to cleave to God. This is meant to be a permanent, everlasting attachment that keeps growing in strength until we become one with God and His Son, Jesus Christ.

The other meaning of the word *cleave* might also be instructive. When we attach ourselves to God, we simultaneously detach ourselves from the adversary. We are separated from evil. The following verse in the New Testament emphasizes the stark line between God and the adversary: "No man can serve two masters: for either he will hate the one, and love the other; or else he will hold [be attached] to the one, and despise the other" (Matthew 6:24). Therefore we must attach ourselves to one or the other. We cannot attach ourselves to both. One attachment cuts the other off or "cleaves it asunder."

In many ways, the world has corrupted the meaning of how a husband and wife become one flesh. Physical intimacy is essential to a healthy eternal marriage but not the type of intimacy that is most often portrayed in the media, which emphasizes the satiation of sexual urges, rather than the intimate union of two marriage partners who have covenanted with each other to love and serve one another. Physical intimacy is not the central meaning of the word *cleave*. As equal partners, sealed together, we make covenants to cleave spiritually and emotionally to each other. That means that we covenant not only to reserve our physical intimacy for our eternal companion, but also our emotional and spiritual intimacy—cleaving with our whole soul to each other and to no one else.

The couple mentioned earlier who came to me for help with their marriage had difficulty cleaving spiritually and emotionally to each other. Their conversations at home must have been quite superficial. They had not established a pattern of sharing their deepest feelings. When their negative talk rose to its peak, I broke in and tried to deflect the tone and reduce the tension. I said, "You know, your words are pretty harsh, so let's rewind your conversation for a moment. I want to hear you tell me why you love each other." A few moments of complete silence ensued, and then the conversation changed significantly. They settled down and began to remember why they had married in the first place. Rather than harshness, their expressions to each other softened, and the feeling in the room markedly changed. Finally, at the end of the session, they embraced each other. Weeks later the husband informed me that their relationship had improved, that they were happier than they had ever been in the marriage, and that they had decided to stay together. Given that they both had avoidant attachment styles, they likely needed therapy following that initial visit to change some of the unhealthy patterns that had damaged their relationship. But they were determined to change, and that is what led them to a happier marriage.

I believe this couple's marriage endured because they refocused themselves on the Lord. They began to remember their temple covenants. When both husband and wife cleave to God—when they base their marriage on the Savior's Atonement—they will cleave to each other in a way that will continually strengthen their relationship. The more they love the Lord, the more they will love each other and their offspring. The more they feel protected by God, the more they will feel protected by each other. The more they trust God, the more they will trust each other. The more they feel accepted and forgiven by God, the more they will feel accepted and forgiven by each other. This is what it means to cleave to one another as eternal companions. No other attachment can match it. It is worth every prayer, every hope, every conversation, every effort we can devote to it.

A happy, healthy, lasting marriage—one that keeps growing and changing, one that enriches and strengthens both partners—is a strong desire of everyone who hopes to have a covenant family in mortality. Every disciple of Christ wants a marriage founded on His teachings, a marriage that draws on His power and on His love. These questions gnaw at most of us: "Can my marriage be that good? Can we create an equal partnership that not only endures but flourishes? Can our love for each other keep growing and never stop?" My own answer is an emphatic yes!

If such a marriage is possible, how do we create it, nurture it, and sustain it? We can begin by reflecting on our own relationship style. Are there elements of avoidance or anxiety in how we relate to others? Or do we naturally form lasting, secure relationships with others? Did we enjoy a healthy attachment to our family members and friends? Has our attachment to God always been positive and strong? What about our spouse or prospective spouse? What was his or her relationship to others and to God? What effects do our spouse's attachments have on our marriage and on our attachment to God?

As a married couple or a couple contemplating marriage, you might review this chart as you ask yourselves the following questions about your relationship:

- Does personal anxiety ever put a strain on your attachment? Do you worry that your spouse does not love you as much as you desire?
- Do you or your spouse ever want to avoid each other due to a momentary lack of trust?
- Do you ever avoid your mate because you don't want to complicate things?
- Do you wish your spouse could provide you with more safety and protection?
- Do you wish your spouse could help you be more creative and take risks that could lead to a more fulfilling and productive life?

If you think it would be helpful, you might talk as a couple about each of these questions and decide what actions both of you might take to help you strengthen your attachment so that you can have a happier, healthier relationship in which each of you is more fully cleaving to your spouse and to God.

Part Two
ATTACHMENT TO GOD

Your Heavenly Father loves you.
That love never changes. . . .
God's love is there for you whether or not
you feel you deserve love.
It is simply always there.[1]

—Thomas S. Monson

It was our second week in Beijing, China. Still trying to adjust to the language and culture, six university students and I entered the great "Gate of China" on our way to tour the Imperial City, a place once forbidden to all but the emperor and his family. Above the gate hung a bigger-than-life portrait of Mao Zedong, the father of the People's Republic of China. One of my students, who I will call Lifen, asked me in her quiet way if I would like to accept a dinner invitation that evening at the home of her aunt and uncle. She explained that it was an unusual invitation because Chinese people (at that time) were not eager, for a variety of reasons, to host Americans in their homes. I accepted the invitation gladly.

Lifen had grown up in Beijing and lived much of her life with her aunt and uncle, so they were almost like parents to her. As a young child she had lived through the Great Chinese Famine and had explained to me one day how all she and her family had to eat was boiled leaves from nearby trees. Her aunt's home was located surprisingly close to Tiananmen Square—only a short walk from the Gate of China. When we arrived, her aunt and uncle greeted us, and she introduced me as her professor. By their almost reverential response, it was obvious that the title "professor" meant much more in China than it did in the U.S. After I had met her aunt and uncle, she introduced me to her two cousins, their teenage sons. I will call the fifteen-year-old Ouyang and the eighteen-year-old Huiliang.

---

1.   Thomas S. Monson, "You Never Walk Alone," *Ensign*, November 2013.

While Lifen's aunt was preparing the meal, Huiliang, a tall, thin, and thoughtful young man, motioned to me to follow him to his bedroom, where he proudly showed me the painting of Christ on his wall. "My grandfather was a Christian," he explained, "and I keep this picture of Jesus on my bedroom wall to honor my grandfather every day." I was shocked to see a picture of the Savior in a Chinese home. This was a country that had prohibited me from bringing any religious materials with me, a country that for decades had drilled into its citizens' minds that there was no God. When meeting with the Dalai Lama, Mao had reportedly said, "Religion is poison." So seeing a picture of Christ on the wall of a young person in China was quite astonishing.

I had noticed that Huliang's younger brother, Ouyang, had not come with us to look at the picture. In fact, when we returned to the kitchen table, he was already seated directly across from me, looking as if he could not wait for the meal to begin. After the food was put before us, Ouyang went into attack mode, which was highly unusual for a young Chinese person. Chinese children and youth are taught from their earliest years to respect adults and to speak only when spoken to. So when Ouyang began his questioning, I was surprised. He peered into my eyes, pointed his finger at my face, and exclaimed, "You cannot prove there is a God!" Because he caught me off guard, I was not sure how to respond.

Rather than becoming defensive, I leaned back in my chair, took hold of my shirt, and said, "See this blue shirt? You can touch it. You can see it. You agree that it exists, right?" Ouyang nodded his head in agreement.

"But you say that because you can't see God, nor touch Him, you cannot believe that He exists."

Again Ouyang nodded.

I then took a picture of my wife from my wallet. "Now let me show you a picture of my wife. This is my wife back in our home in the U.S. We've been married for a long time and have five children. Do you believe that she exists?"

"Sure, but that's different," Ouyang retorted. "She's alive. You have seen her and know her. That's different than God."

"Okay, that is a little different. I agree. But let me tell you something about her. She loves me, and I love her. I can't see that love. I can't touch it, but I know that it exists just as surely as I know that this blue shirt exists."

At this point Ouyang retreated slightly.

"Now, Ouyang, I wonder if you and Huiliang will come back into the bedroom with me." They agreed. When we arrived back in the bedroom, I asked them to look at the picture of Christ on the wall. "The main reason I believe that Christ came to earth—that He was a real person and that He still lives—is because I feel His love for me every day. He is not with me physically, but He is with me spiritually. I know because He loves me."

Ouyang became a little more pensive. I'm sure that he had looked at that picture his whole life, but he could never understand how his grandfather could believe in a being he could not see or touch. Huiliang seemed genuinely grateful for the explanation, as if he already had the seeds of belief inside.

As children we learn the song "I Feel My Savior's Love." But as adults we may feel His love in new and different ways. No one in Lifen's family that day in China could have affirmed Christ's love for them. If they had felt it, they did not know how to label or identify it as divine love. Lifen once confided, "I've tried to believe in God, but I just can't. I've had too many years of believing that He does not exist, and I don't know how to change that."

Some are like my Chinese friend Lifen—they have difficulty ever recognizing the existence of a supreme being. This inability to feel God's love or to recognize His existence may be traced back to a child's inability to feel a close secure attachment to parents. As some research has shown, "Attachment-related differences affect religious experience and development. Secure attachment with parents predicted subsequent re-affirmation of their parents' faith."[2] I am not, of course, asserting that all faith crises are the results of problematic parental attachment. Some children who have experienced the most stable and healthy parental attachments may still pull away from the Church, from God, or from both. The point is that parent-child relationships should be nurtured throughout one's life, and if a child departs from the covenant path, strengthening the parent-child relationship, regardless of how strong it is already, will be a blessing to both parent and child.

Many people have felt God's presence at least some point in their lives, but when trials or doubts come, their faith weakens and they begin to wonder if their belief was just wishful thinking. This happened to another acquaintance of mine. He had been active in the Church for many years, but then his faith began to waver. While explaining why he had become less active, my friend said, "I came to a point when I wondered if what I'd been taught all my life was true—that when you kept the commandments, God would help you. But I felt I was keeping the commandments, and I didn't feel that I was receiving any help at all. I felt abandoned and forgotten. That's when I began to struggle with my testimony."

I asked him what had helped him return to activity. He explained,

> I knew that I loved God. I knew that He loved me—even though I was having a hard time feeling that love. So I kept going. I kept searching. And one day I could see that there was no perfect correlation between my keeping the commandments and blessings I lacked. It was a little bit like the rich man who came to Jesus and asked what he needed to do to follow the Savior. And the Savior told him to sell everything. I didn't have an attachment to material things. That was not my problem, but I was not yet willing

---

2.   Aaron D. Cherniak, Mario Mikulincer, Phillip R. Shaver, and Pehr Granqvist, "Attachment Theory and Religion," *ScienceDirect 40*: 126–130, https://www.sciencedirect.com/science/article/pii/S2352250X2030172X.

to give myself fully to God. I was holding back. When I stopped holding out and holding back, His love seemed to surround me as never before. I could not deny it. That's when I decided I was wrong to keep looking for the evidence of blessings I was expecting. That's when I became determined to give my all to the Lord.

Feeling God's love is as essential to our spiritual life as air is to our physical life. The question I ask myself is, how I can feel His love more deeply, more often, more fully? How I can literally be filled with His love? I can never be content with my current status. I must always be progressing. It is impossible, after all, to experience too much of God's love, as it is impossible for me to love Him too much. I want to always find ways to increase my capacity to love Him and to receive His love in return. I want to watch continually that I don't distance myself even for a brief time from the Lord as did my friend or fall into the adversary's trap of disbelief as did my Chinese friends. No, I must always hope, pray, and act in ways that will lead to a closer attachment with the One who loves me infinitely and eternally.

CLEAVING TO GOD

*Come with full purpose of heart, and cleave
unto God as he cleaveth unto you.*

—Jacob 6:5

Our attachment to our earthly parents is paramount in our development as humans in mortality, but our attachment to God is even more crucial to our well-being. This is an attachment that those in the secular world either do not recognize or seldom mention. It supersedes all other relationships and affects the quality of each attachment we form in this life. It obviously goes beyond this life. We loved God before we came to earth and will love Him even more when we return to His presence after this life. He is our Rock, our solace, our rest. We may choose to forsake Him for a moment or for a lifetime, but He "will never, no never forsake" us.[1]

The following diagram is similar to the one shown in the previous chapter on marital attachment, but in this case we are focusing on our attachment to God. Just as our goal in marriage is to be securely attached to our eternal companion, our goal in our relationship with Divinity is to have a secure attachment to

---

1. "How Firm a Foundation," *Hymns of The Church of Jesus Christ of Latter-day Saints* (Salt Lake City, Utah: The Church of Jesus Christ of Latter-day Saints, 1985).

God—the feeling of loving God with all our heart, as shown in the upper left quadrant of the diagram.

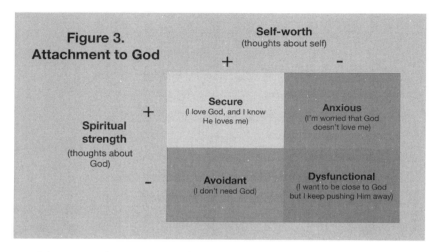

That attachment can form when we understand our personal worth—that we are literally His sons and His daughters. Then our thoughts about our Father in Heaven and His Son Jesus Christ will lead to an increasing sense of spiritual strength. The attachment described in the upper left quadrant is a healthy attachment—one that lasts and keeps growing. The old English meaning of the word *health* is "to be healed, to be righteous, to be safe." When one is righteous, healed, and safe, one is cleaving tightly to God.

The friend I mentioned who became less active for a period of time had momentarily stopped cleaving to the Lord and lost his healthy divine attachment. When our self-worth suffers, we may worry that God no longer loves us because we aren't worth loving, or so we think. In this case our attachment is anxious as shown in the upper right quadrant. I have known people with this kind of attachment. One said to me, "I know God can save me, but I really don't think I'm worth saving. I've done too many bad things." Sin distances us from God, so when we sin, we don't feel close to Him. Then, like this individual, we might even think it is impossible to regain the closeness we so much desire.

The lower right quadrant shows the dysfunctional attachment. In this type of attachment the person strongly desires to be close to God but then paradoxically pushes Him away, seldom thinking about Him, feeling His love, or expecting to feel close to Him. We are all supposed to "fear" God, but the fear that the scriptures urge us to have is a reverence for Him, not a fear that He will punish us or desert us. Those with a dysfunctional attachment style know that God exists. However, they do not trust that God knows that they exist or that He accepts them, so their fear causes them to push God away from them. This might be termed an emotional-spiritual disorder.

We all have moments when we feel deserted, forgotten, or ignored. Even those closest to us may not understand what we need. And the more we try to explain what we need, the more confused we may become. At times we simply don't know what we need. God, however, knows precisely what we need. He has known us for eons. He understands our longings, our frustrations, our hopes, and our desires. His attachment to us is constant, but our attachment to Him can vary as we face the ups and downs of mortality.

I had a friend whose wife decided to leave him and pursue another path. He pled with her to stay, but she was immovable. Following the separation (the detachment), his emotions flew all around. At times he was resolved to coax her back; at other times he was angry with her, and then feelings of relief would come. I asked him about his relationship with God during this trying period of his life. He paused a minute and then said, "I was never angry at God, but I found myself questioning Him. Why did He allow our marriage to crumble like that?" Then he continued with what I found to be insightful: "So at times I felt the Lord was far away, like maybe He had forgotten me. But then my logic set in. I knew down deep He had not deserted me, but I had a hard time feeling His love."

When mortal attachments weaken in mortality, attachment to God often weakens as well—not because God's love has diminished in any way but because our ability to feel His love has diminished. Research has shown that children with distant or abusive fathers have difficulty believing in God and feeling His love.[2] The pain that abusive or neglectful fathers cause confronts us often. A friend recently recounted to me an experience he had while trying to help young men who had been placed in a special school for troubled youth.

> I could see that these young men did not really understand that they were valued and loved, so I gave a talk on what it means to be a child of God. As I was speaking, I could see that they were not responding as I had hoped. Following the talk I asked the counselor what went wrong. He said, "Nearly all of these boys grew up with abusive fathers; nothing could be more frightening or alien to them than the idea of a male-figure god. They could never trust their fathers, so how could they trust God?"

The counselor went on to describe the connection between Radical Attachment Disorder and the emotional, social, and spiritual deficits that nearly all the residents of the school were experiencing.

Those whose spouse or closest friend deserts them likewise have difficulty feeling the presence of God in their lives. Desertion by a loved one can cause us to distance ourselves from the very one who could console us in our darkest moment. Those who experience anxiety—either because they feel unworthy or because they are afraid of being deserted—are quite different from those in the lower left quadrant who, rather than feeling anxious, feel overly

---

2. Alicia Limke-McLean, "Attachment to God: Differentiating the Contributions of Fathers and Mothers Using the Experiences in Parental Relationships Scale," *Journal of Psychology and Theology*, 2014, https://www.researchgate.net/profile/Alicia_Limke-Mclean/publication/230584273_Attachment_to_God_Differentiating_the_Contributions_of_Fathers_and_Mothers_Using_the_Experiences_in_Parental_Relationships_Scale/links/09e41501aad5c082ad000000/Attachment-to-God-Differentiating-the-Contributions-of-Fathers-and-Mothers-Using-the-Experiences-in-Parental-Relationships-Scale.pdf?origin=publication_detail

confident in their own ability to live life without God. They avoid trying to form an attachment with Him because they simply do not see the need.

When I was a mission president, one of our missionaries recounted an experience tracting in an upscale neighborhood. When the elders rang the doorbell, a woman opened the door and said somewhat sarcastically, "So you came to teach me about God. Is that right?" The missionaries nodded their heads. She then invited them into her home. They looked at the curving staircase descending onto a large entryway with a marble floor and were somewhat overcome with the size and beauty of her home. In a berating tone, the woman said, "I want you to take a look at this home. I've got all that I need. Why would you think that I need God?" Then she asked the missionaries to leave. She had an avoidant attitude toward God, along with an avoidant feeling toward the missionaries.

Our attachment to God affects all other relationships in our lives. One who feels distant from God often has difficulty feeling close to a parent, a spouse, or a friend. That is precisely why loving God is the first and great commandment. If we can receive and reciprocate God's love, then we can receive and reciprocate others' love. This supremely important attachment affects all others.

The person who is in the lower left quadrant (avoidant) feels little need for God, for a spouse, or for a friend. Those in the anxious quadrant are not only fearful that God will desert them, but they're fearful that a parent, a spouse, or a friend will desert them as well. Relationships are intertwined with each other. Researchers have shown that those who have a distant relationship with their father have much more difficulty drawing close to God. The kind of attachment one has with one's father has significant impact on the kind of attachment one has with God.[3]

---

3. Richard K. Hart, "The Marriage Metaphor," *Ensign*, January 1995, https://www.churchofjesuschrist.org/study/ensign/1995/01/the-marriage-metaphor?lang=eng.

When one feels loved by parents, one is much more likely to feel loved by God. Parental love gives us feelings of safety, security, and strength, and God's love is similar. The Lord provides us a safe haven through His mercy—His infinite power to forgive us when we falter. He provides us with a secure base through His grace—His enabling power—that helps us know we can accomplish our mission here on earth, even when it may seem far beyond our grasp. A friend once explained to me that our doctrine of grace is richer and more far reaching than most of us realize. "We believe not only in the grace of the Savior Jesus Christ, but in the grace of the Father as well. By His grace God the Father gave us spiritual life, he provided for us the Plan of Salvation and permitted His Son to die for us so that the Plan could be accomplished. So in the Restored Church of Jesus Christ we are doubly blessed with the power of God's grace in our lives because we feel the grace of both the Father and the Son."[4]

Those who speak of the importance of attachments in our lives usually base their findings on human relationships alone. They see a parent's capacity to provide a safe haven and secure base for a child emanating from the inner strength of the parent, but as members of the Church of Jesus Christ, we have a far deeper, far more compelling understanding of attachment. We know that someone's power to show mercy to another, to help that person feel safe and protected comes from a loving Father in Heaven and His Son, Jesus Christ, and that the ability to empower another person to reach beyond what seems possible at the time draws upon the Father and Son's grace—their enabling power to lift us higher and magnify us more than we might ever have imagined.

The secure enduring attachment with God we seek creates in us the capacity not only to endure our own trials but to form attachments with others that will help them overcome *their* trials. The parent who forgives a child, the husband and wife who

---

4. Joseph F. McConkie, personal communication, 2003.

forgive each other, and the friend who sees beyond the other's failings are acting not only on their own abilities but on divine power. When we allow our relationship with God to influence all of our actions, both the giver and the receiver are blessed by divine mercy and grace. The giver's and receiver's attachment to God grows stronger as they give and receive divine love to one another. As the attachment with God the Father and His Son Jesus Christ becomes stronger, we will be more able to help others strengthen their own attachments.

Amulek's experience helps us see this principle more clearly. Amulek had distanced himself from God, perhaps becoming more attached to his material possessions than he was to the Lord, but at a moment when his heart was softened he received a heavenly message from an angel—perhaps the same angel who had recently visited Alma and instructed him to return to the land of Ammonihah. Because Amulek received the angel's message and obeyed the instructions, he immediately recognized that Alma was indeed a prophet and invited Alma to his home. That meeting—that budding friendship that had been initiated by heavenly intervention—became a strong attachment between two devoted servants of the Lord. They traveled together, preached together, and baptized together, heeding the angelic promptings that had come to them.

As Amulek and Alma preached the gospel and baptized people unto repentance, they not only strengthened their own attachment to God but to each other as well. Their attachment to God—which was just developing in Amulek—nurtured their mortal friendship in a way that was made possible by their closeness to the Spirit. Alma's devotion surely increased Amulek's devotion to the Savior and His divine mission to bring salvation and exhalation to all His children. And as they brought the message of the gospel to the people, they opened the way for every one of those newly converted members to strengthen their own attachment to God and to each other.

It is no coincidence that the gospel is preached today "two by two." It is also no coincidence that the relationships that form between companions are a strong determinant of the success of missionary companionships. If the relationship is strained, the work will suffer, but as the attachment strengthens, the missionaries' ability to help those they teach to feel the Holy Spirit increases. When my wife and I received a call to preside over a mission, a former companion of mine called me to congratulate me on the new assignment. "I always knew you would someday be a mission president!" he exclaimed. He continued to express confidence in me that we would succeed in what at that moment appeared to be a daunting assignment. After the call ended, I told my wife, "That was my trainer—my first companion as a nineteen-year-old missionary. He's still my trainer. I've had so little contact with him since the mission, but he is still trying to build me up so that I can do well in this calling."

Missionaries who train their companions are simply extending the Lord's grace or the enabling power of the Savior's Atonement. They are building, strengthening, and lifting their companion to meet the demands of a divinely inspired call. And that is what we all do with each other: ministering sisters and ministering brothers, co-workers, mentors, friends, family members, and especially parents are the same. An observant friend remarked, "Everybody needs a missionary!" Everyone needs someone close to them who is building, strengthening, and lifting them so that they can accomplish what first seems impossible—to do what they really want to do but could not do without some outside help.

Our attachment with God helps us know when, how, and to whom we need to reach out. It helps us know how to let others into our lives, how to forgive them when they make mistakes, and how to love them in spite of their humanness. Machines can do things flawlessly, humans cannot. Because we are human, we need divine power to enrich our relationships. When the Savior's power infuses our attachments we feel renewed, enlivened, and hopeful. We are reassured that a moment of discord will dissolve into a lifetime of love and an eternity of joy.

As you've been reading, what thoughts have come to you about your own attachment to God? Is it as strong as you would like it to be? Are you actively trying to strengthen it? If so, in what ways? And what about your family members and close friends? Are any of them struggling with their attachment to God? If so, have thoughts come to you about what you might do to help them find more faith in the Lord and feel His love more fully in their lives?

SCRIPTURAL SYMBOLS

For thy Maker is thine husband;
the Lord of hosts is his name;
and thy Redeemer the Holy One of Israel;
The God of the whole earth shall be called.

—Isaiah 54:5

Someone might ask, what is the central purpose of the restored gospel of Jesus Christ? Is its purpose to help us be kind to one another? Yes, but how does living the gospel do that? Is its purpose to help us receive all of the saving ordinances? Yes, but why are those ordinances so essential? Is its purpose to help us give up our fallen nature and learn how to be righteous? Yes, but again, how does that happen?

I believe the central purpose of the Restoration is to help us learn how to become one with our Father in Heaven and His Son, Jesus Christ. How do we do that? By becoming His sons and His daughters and being filled with His love. Only then will we be able to see Him as He is (see Moroni 7:48). Only then will we be able to return to His presence. The purpose of the restored gospel might be summed up in one word: *attachment*. Attachment is why the first commandment is the most important. The more we love Him, the more tightly we are bound to Him, the more we will become like Him, and the more we will be filled with His love. The more we are filled with His love, the more we will love

His children. And the more we love His children, the more we will serve them, succor them, forgive them, and help them come along the path we are striving to travel.

One might wonder, if the word *attachment* is so accurate in conveying the central purpose of the gospel of Jesus Christ, why is it found in the Bible Dictionary and Topical Guide but not in the scriptures themselves? *Attachment* is actually a word that has been used for centuries, but it was first used as a legal term in reference to an individual's property: "writ of attachment." The meaning we ascribe to the word—devotion to someone or something or fondness or affection for another person—is a more recent use of the word, particularly as it relates to familial relationships. However, even though the word *attachment* does not appear in the scriptures, the concept of fondness or affection or devotion to another—especially to God—appears frequently. For example, the commandment "Thou shalt have no other God before me" (Mosiah 12:35) makes it clear that we should be attached to God and not let anything take the place of that attachment. We are further taught that "every man walketh after the image of his own god, whose image is in the likeness of the world" (D&C 1:16). This is another warning not to allow anything, no matter how appealing the world might make it appear, to come between us and God.

To understand the centrality of our attachment to God, we need to recognize the symbols and metaphors of this attachment as we read the standard works. For example, we know that God the Father is literally the father of our spirits. We do not see this as a symbol but as an actual relationship we have with God. But the scriptures also refer to Christ as our father, which is more symbolic in nature. We are His children because we take upon us His name, worship Him, and follow His example. We are of the house of Israel, His covenant children. He is the One who frees us from the captivity of death and sin, because He loves us as a parent loves a child.

The baptismal ordinance is symbolic of Christ's death, burial, and resurrection, so as we participate in this ordinance we become one with the Savior—we strengthen our attachment to Him. The sacrament is an ordinance of attachment. We eat bread that represents the Savior's flesh and drink water that represents His blood. It is a renewal of those same covenants of attachment that we made at the time we were baptized. Similarly all other covenants can be viewed as means of strengthening our attachment to God the Father and His Son, Jesus Christ.

The scriptures are rich with metaphors that point to our attachment to God. They liken Christ to the bridegroom—the one who is attached to us as firmly and eternally as a husband is to his wife. Old Testament prophets similarly taught that the Savior is a "husband" to us as members of His Church (see Isaiah 54:5; Jeremiah 31:32). This metaphor continues in the New Testament (see Matthew 25:1), as well as in modern-day scripture (see D&C 65:3; 88:92). Jesus always used metaphors that were familiar to those He was teaching, so these comparisons of Himself to a bridegroom or husband or the father of the house of Israel were the most basic, fundamental relationship metaphors that He could possibly have used.

The metaphor of the vine and the branches is also used to help us understand the closeness of our relationship with the Savior.[1] "I am the true vine, and my Father is the husbandman. Abide in me, and I in you. As the branch cannot bear fruit of itself, except it abide in the vine; no more can ye, except ye abide in me" (John 15:1, 4). What more descriptive metaphor could Jesus have used to show that we are attached to Him than to depict how a branch is attached to the vine—not any vine, but the true vine? As with most good metaphors, the meaning can continue to be unpacked as one thinks about how the parent vine nourishes the branches, gives life to them, and how the "husbandman" or God

---

1.   Anthony R. Temple, *Parables of Jesus: I Am the True Vine,* The Church of Jesus Christ of Latter-day Saints.

the Father cares for the vineyard, nourishing the soil around the vine, watering it so it can grow and give life to each branch. If the branches of the vine receive the nourishment that comes to them through Christ, then they will flourish. But if they refuse the nourishment, they will wither and may need pruning to survive.

Similarly the scriptures teach that we should be "grounded, rooted, established, and settled" just as a healthy plant is.[2] Our attachment to our Father in Heaven and His Son, Jesus Christ, needs to be so solid, so unyielding that we cannot be uprooted as an unhealthy plant might be. Our roots need to go deep. That means learning all we can about the Savior, His mission, and our role in that mission. It means coming to rely on our Heavenly Father because our faith in His Son is settled, never wavering. So we come to see ourselves as children of Israel, attached by the Abrahamic covenant to the Lord.

How might you more fully experience the power of scriptural symbols by considering the following?

Receive and reflect on sacred ordinances.
Reflect on how sacred symbols can help you draw closer to God and to others.
Welcome the nourishment, the pruning, and the love.
Imagine being more grounded, rooted, established, and settled.

---

2. Neal A. Maxwell. September 15, 1981. Grounded, Rooted, Established, and Settled. BYU Speeches https://speeches.byu.edu/talks/neal-a-maxwell/grounded-rooted-established-settled/

COMMANDMENTS

*We cannot truly love God if we do not love
our fellow travelers on this mortal journey.
Likewise, we cannot fully love our fellowmen
if we do not love God, the Father of us all.*[1]

—Thomas S. Monson

The entire Christian world thinks of the Ten Commandments as a broad set of guidelines for living the way God wants us to live—a moral code—but many may not realize that all Ten Commandments focus on relationships. The first four emphasize our relationship with God. The final six focus on our relationships with His children. They can be considered as the Ten Commandments of Relationships (or Attachments) because they are all based on what it means to love in healthy ways that lead to happiness now and in eternity.

Our Attachment to God

The first commandment urges us to place God first in our lives (see Exodus 20:3). As stated in the Doctrine and Covenants 59:5,

---

1. Thomas S. Monson, "Love—The Essence of the Gospel," *Ensign*, May 2014, 91.

"Thou shalt love the Lord thy God with all thy heart, with all thy might, mind, and strength; and in the name of Jesus Christ thou shalt serve Him." We look to God continually throughout the day. This commandment indicates that no other relationship should preempt or diminish our relationship with God. All we do and all we say can be an expression of our love for the Father of our spirit and His Son, Jesus Christ.

The second of the Ten Commandments expands upon the first: "Thou shalt not make unto thee any graven image" (Exodus 20:4). No object should come between us and God. We worship God and God alone. Although we have a relationship with money, material goods, food, and the environment (all of God's creations) we can never allow any of these to come between us and our creator. We can never allow ourselves to become attached to these outward things. Our preeminent attachment must be to God, who gave us spiritual life before we came to earth.

The third commandment asks that we address our Father in Heaven in reverence—never to "take His name in vain" (Exodus 20:7). Even though the world refers to God in reckless, sacrilegious, or profane terms, we keep His name holy in the way we address Him in prayer and in our unspoken thoughts throughout the day. We would never speak of a loved one in a reckless or profane way. We speak of those we love in terms of the closeness of attachment. And so it is with the Lord.

On the surface, keeping the Sabbath day holy may not appear to be a relationship commandment, but I believe it is (see Exodus 20:8). The way we spend our time on the Sabbath day is an extremely important way we communicate our love to the Lord. It is His day, and we offer our oblations (our sacrifices, our broken heart, and contrite spirit) to Him, much the same as a husband might communicate his love for his wife by focusing on her needs rather than on his own. As President Nelson has taught: "When I had to make a decision whether or not an activity was appropriate for the Sabbath, I simply asked myself, 'What sign do I want to give to God?'" He knew that by his conduct he could show the Lord how much he loved Him.[2]

Our Attachment to Others

When the lawyer asked Jesus which was the greatest of all the commandments, Jesus summarized all ten of them in only two "great commandments": Love the Lord and love thy neighbor. So, our overall purpose in mortality is to increase our capacity to love God and love all of His children. Six of the commandments remind us how we might achieve such an increase. As we consider these commandments, we must remember that they are all subordinate to the first and great commandment to love God. Our attachment to Him is included in all other attachments we have in life. When we think about any of the final six commandments, we need to understand how our love for God affects all relationships in mortality.

The fifth commandment, for example, asks us to honor our parents—the first attachment we experience in this life (see Exodus 20:12). It is a parental attachment, like our attachment to our Heavenly Parents. It has always been easy for me to honor my parents. They were stable, consistent followers of Christ, but some may have parents who do not merit much honor and respect. Such parental relationships can make it difficult for children to develop close attachments with others and can also damage heavenly attachments.

I once spoke with a young man who had six different fathers prior to serving his mission. He explained, "My mother would divorce one and then marry another one and another one. Each of my fathers, including my birth father, was abusive in some way. Just before my mission, my stepfather would come into my bedroom to wake me up. He would look down at me as if he was

---

2.   Russell M. Nelson, "The Sabbath Is a Delight," *Ensign*, May 2015.

totally disgusted with me, and say, 'You are a loser, a real loser! I would just look back at him, say nothing, and get out of bed.'"

I asked this young man how he overcame the effects of abuse. He had difficulty describing how the abuse had affected him and what he had done to get beyond it and prepare to serve a mission. Most of his comments focused on how people other than his parents had stepped in and helped him.

Abuse, neglect, and rejection unfortunately affect many children and youth. While serving as a Church leader, I once met with a young woman who was planning to serve a mission. As we talked about her physical health, she described how she had struggled with anorexia for several years and how her doctors were concerned about her ability to serve a mission at that point. When I asked her if she had experienced any form of sexual abuse as a child, she appeared shocked at my question. "How did you know?" I told her that I had not known if she had been abused, but I did know that those with anorexia (bulimic syndrome) had a much higher probability of having had childhood sexual abuse than those in the general population.[3] I explained that I had asked her that question because I wanted to know if she had ever received counseling for the trauma caused by the abuse.

I have often thought how difficult it is for those who have been abused or neglected to truly honor their parents as the fifth commandment requires. Certainly they do not need to honor their parents' behavior, but eventually they need to forgive them for the mistreatment. One woman told a powerful story of how she forgave her abusive father. She said, "I knew forgiveness didn't mean condoning or accepting the abuse or forgetting that it had occurred. It meant I needed to take what I could from life's experiences and through the

---

3. Lena Sanci, Carolyn Coffey, and Craig Olsson, "Childhood Sexual Abuse and Eating Disorders in Females: Findings from the Victorian Adolescent Health Cohort Study," *JAMA Pediatrics*, 2008 162: 261-267. https://jama-network.com/journals/jamapediatrics/fullarticle/379204

Atonement of Jesus Christ and the grace of God, find healing and forgiveness. Forgiveness didn't come in one 'warm fuzzy' moment either. It came gradually, over decades. Time is a great healer."[4]

While the fifth commandment is a positive injunction to honor our parents, the sixth commandment is negatively stated—it commands that we shall not kill (see Exodus 20:13). At first glance this might seem like the one we don't need to worry about. I do not wake up in the morning wondering whether I will commit murder, and likely neither do you. Not a hard commandment to keep, we might think. But 1 John 3:15 states: "Whosoever hateth his brother is a murderer." Wait a minute, how can that be? Is it saying that my emotions can kill even if I don't have a gun, even if I don't pull the trigger? The scriptures teach that anger alone is akin to killing (see Matthew 5:22).

Emmanuel Levinas, a French Jewish philosopher, asserted that the very essence of our humanness can be found in how we respond to the face of "the Other," who is anyone we encounter. He describes the "face" as the most vulnerable part of the body, the part that is open to view. He further explains that the unspoken word of every face of every person we meet is, "Thou shalt not kill." In other words, "Whatever you, the stranger, might do, please don't hurt me." But the face of the Other also says, "Please help me."

In Levinas' words: "The first word of the face is 'Thou shalt not kill.' It is an order. There is a commandment in the appearance of the face, as if a master spoke to me. However, at the same time, the face of the Other is destitute; it is the poor for whom I can do all and to whom I owe all."[5]

As a friend once said to me, "When it is not sought, advice can be an act of violence."

---

4. Name withheld, "Learning to Forgive" *Ensign*, March, 2011.
5. Emmanuel Levinas, *Ethics and Infinity* (Pittsburgh, PA: Duquesne University Press, 1985), 89.

So, the sixth commandment may not be so simple after all. I have heard people say, "Oh, it's healthy to express anger. It helps you get rid of negative feelings." Relationships demand that we speak the truth to each other, but not with harshness, vindictiveness, or vengeance. The scriptures are clear: We are not only commanded to avoid killing someone, but we are also commanded to avoid lashing out at them in anger. President Russell M. Nelson and his wife Wendy have spoken often of the need to avoid contention of any kind in the home, even contention that is portrayed in media. Anger breeds contention, and contention often heightens anger, which can make it impossible for us to receive inspiration from God.[6]

The seventh commandment—thou shalt not commit adultery—used to be punishable by law. Now it is much more accepted. When the Lord commanded us to avoid doing "anything like unto it" (D&C 59:6), He was trying to protect us from the emotional and spiritual pain that inevitably comes from breaking our marriage covenant. Because marriage is a covenant relationship—one that is solemnized in the temple—our responsibility to remain true is especially critical. Our spouse is not just any "other": we have vowed to become one with our spouse, just as we become one with God. The positive side of this commandment is that husband and wife are commanded to be intimate with each other to help create that oneness, but that intimacy must be reserved for the eternal companion. Such intimacy extends beyond the physical relationship. Emotional intimacy must also be reserved for those who have made the marriage covenant. We seek fidelity in marriage, and we also seek it in our relationship with the Lord. We want to be faithful, trustable, and consistent in our discipleship.

This understanding leads to the eighth commandment: "Thou shalt not steal." This commandment is usually associated with theft

---

6 . Sarah Jane Weaver, "Episode 12: Sister Wendy Nelson joins Sister Sheri Dew to talk about President Nelson's 3 years as Prophet," *Church News*, January 5, 2021, https://www.thechurchnews.com/podcast/2021-01-05/sister-wendy-nelson-sheri-dew-president-nelson-prophet-three-years-201007

of some type of property, which obviously can have negative effects on a relationship. Property, however, can be returned or replaced. I recall a young man coming to me with a desire to repent for stealing a portable sound system from an electronics store. Since he was unable to physically visit the store and return the merchandise he had stolen, he said, "So I've been thinking of writing a letter and apologizing for my mistake." I responded, "That's a good idea. And I assume you'll reimburse the store owner for the cost of the sound system." He appeared shocked at what I had said and responded, "I thought the letter would be enough." I then explained that the letter was only part of the process; he also needed to give back or pay for what he had stolen.

Property theft is a much simpler sin to rectify than other types of stealing. One can steal hope from another person, confidence, or even faith. A friend or family member can draw me closer to God simply by being in my presence, strengthening my attachment to Deity. But someone might also do the opposite—cause another to doubt God, weaken a person's faith, and thereby weaken their attachment to our Father in Heaven. This is a much more serious type of stealing than the theft of property. Theft of money, for example, causes momentary loss, but theft of another person's faith can have eternal consequences.

The ninth commandment instructs us not to lie—not to bear false witness. Nothing strengthens an attachment more than complete honesty, and perhaps nothing can weaken an attachment more than a lie. Marriage relationships, friendships, sibling relationships, and most significantly our relationship with God must be based on complete honesty. I have always been interested in the different ways members respond to the temple recommend questions. They often respond with a quick and sure "Yes" to many of the questions, but when asked if they are honest, they often pause and say something like, "I hope so," "I think I am," or "I try to be." The latest version of the temple recommend questions now asks, "Do you *strive* to be honest in all that you do?"

Being honest with others and with God has clear implications for the quality of our attachments with them, but what about being honest with ourselves? Sometimes we lie to ourselves. We justify our misbehavior, or we discount our own divine gifts. Either way, rationalizing our weaknesses or ignoring our God-given strengths can have far-reaching negative effects on our relationships. When we justify our own sin, we distance ourselves from God, and when we fail to recognize our own gifts, we can fall short of our divine destiny, a destiny that is founded on our ability to love one another.

Honesty is not a black and white trait or behavior. One can always be more truthful and more forthright, just as one can always be more loving. Knowing how to say the right thing at the right time in the right way is the challenge. Thus, honesty is more than stating a fact; it often demands that we say something in a way that the other person will understand without being hurt. Honesty is a nuanced human trait, one that must be fostered throughout life. Clarity of communication is certainly an aspect of honesty, but the clarity must be bathed in charity. Correction or suggestion needs to come with an "increase of love" (D&C 121:43). The more honest we are, the healthier will be our attachment to God and to others.

The tenth commandment—"thou shalt not covet"—is qualitatively different from the other nine. In this commandment we learn that our actions are not all that matter. To covet is not an action; it's a thought, a feeling that can lead to actions. So while the seventh commandment admonishes us not to commit adultery, the tenth says that we should not even lust after someone. Given the internet-dominated environment in which we now live, one might conclude that even with all the sexual sin that is reported daily on the news, lust in all its forms may be much more common. Perhaps for every sexual assault or every act of infidelity, there are thousands of lustful thoughts.

To covet is to wish for something that one does not have. We might covet others' material possessions, but we might also covet their attractiveness. To want what one cannot have is debilitating and destructive. It leads to self-loathing and depression, as well as to criminal actions. This tenth commandment actually ties to all of the other commandments. Covetousness can precede the act of theft or lying, adultery, or even killing. It's the single most powerful precursor to all kinds of sin. If we can control our impulse to covet, we will drastically reduce our inclination to break any of the other commandments. Lust can cause one to lie, steal, kill, commit adultery, or forget God—it is simply the most common motive behind all that is evil, all that we want to avoid in life. Lust is the complete opposite of love. Elder Jeffrey R. Holland has taught, "Love makes us instinctively reach out to God and other people. Lust, on the other hand, is anything but godly and celebrates self-indulgence. Love comes with open hands and open heart; lust comes with only an open appetite."[7]

The following chart shows how obedience (keeping the commandments) affects our attachment to God.

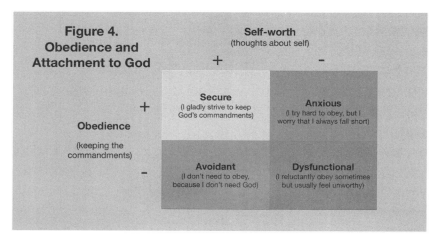

Figure 4. Obedience and Attachment to God

	Self-worth (thoughts about self)	
	+	−
Obedience (keeping the commandments) +	**Secure** (I gladly strive to keep God's commandments)	**Anxious** (I try hard to obey, but I worry that I always fall short)
−	**Avoidant** (I don't need to obey, because I don't need God)	**Dysfunctional** (I reluctantly obey sometimes but usually feel unworthy)

7. Jeffrey R. Holland, "Place No More for the Enemy of My Soul," *Ensign*, May 2010.

Those with a secure attachment style strive to keep God's commandments with gladness and gratitude for the security that comes from such obedience. Those with an anxious style try hard to obey but worry that they can never measure up, that they are always falling short of what God expects of them. Those in the lower right quadrant, "Dysfunctional," seldom obey the Lord and feel increasingly unworthy because of their disobedience. And those with an avoidant style see the commandments as unnecessary constraints that hem them in and hold them back from doing what they want to do. Therefore they feel no need to obey.

Our relationships with God and with others depend on our willingness and eagerness to obey. Consider how keeping each of the Ten Commandments can help us form lasting, healthy, stable attachments with God and with others. It is not coincidental that while Moses was receiving the Ten Commandments in vision on the top of Mount Sinai, the Israelites were participating in wild orgies and making a graven image of a new god made from molten gold (see Exodus 32). They were breaking perhaps all of the commandments they were about to receive from the Lord through their prophet, Moses. Their relationships with each other and with God had been based on lust, lust for sexual pleasure, and lust for material goods. Their conduct reminds us how our attachments to each other are so closely tied to our attachment to God. When one type of relationship suffers, so does the other.

However, the opposite is also true: When our interpersonal relationships are full of love instead of lust, our relationship with God strengthens. We look to Him for guidance—for ways to help us work through the difficulties we face in our attachments to family or friends. And the more we look to Him for help, the closer we move to Him and the more we love Him. This is the great key to unlocking relationship problems. The closer we come to God, the more we love Him and feel His love, and the more we feel His love, the more our capacity grows to share that love with others.

Russell T. Osguthorpe

Which commandment do you consider to be the most difficult for you to obey? How might keeping this commandment draw you closer to God. How might keeping this commandment draw you closer to others?

COVENANTS

Keeping covenants protects us, prepares us,
and empowers us.[1]

—Rosemary M. Wixom

If commandments are the life-blood of attachment, then covenants are the flesh and bone—the connective tissue. Nothing can create attachments as strong and enduring as making and keeping covenants with God. A covenant is more than an agreement, a contract, or a promise. These temporary arrangements are between two people. Covenants are made between God and His children. A promise, for example, is almost always made in relation to time. It is made for a specific event, and when that event ends, the promise ends or is replaced by another temporary promise.

Consider a promise ring that couples in some cultures give to each other. The practice of giving promise rings began in the Middle Ages to show that a couple was dating exclusively. A poetic phrase was often inscribed on the ring, such as "united hearts, death only parts."[2] Even the phrase itself proclaims that this ring

1. Rosemary M. Wixom, "Keeping Covenants Protects, Prepares, and Empowers Us," *Ensign,* November 2014.
2. Gemological Institute of America, *A Guide to Promise Ring Meaning: The Promise Behind the Promise Rings*, 2020, https://4cs.gia.edu/en-us/blog/guide-to-promise-ring-meaning/

is a promise for this life only. The ring could signify commitment but not necessarily commitment to become engaged or even to marry—it was a commitment that for a specified time the couple were promising to date exclusively. If the dating did not yield the hoped for relationship, then the engagement ring would not be given, and the couple would not get married.

In contrast, a covenant relationship, is the most beautiful, transcendent attachment that can be formed on earth or in eternity. Covenants are made between an individual and God when we agree to carry out the conditions the Lord has set for us. The baptismal covenant, for example, is "a new and everlasting covenant" we make when we freely choose to link ourselves with the Lord, to take upon us His name, and to follow His example. It is a covenant that lifts us closer to the Lord, and when paired with the Gift of the Holy Ghost it helps us feel His love more fully and listen to His promptings more completely (see D&C 22).

One of my first companions in the mission field was one of the most impressive missionaries I have ever met. Elder Larsen had a buoyant spirit that combined in a unique way with an inner conviction that he could do whatever the Lord had asked him to do, no matter how challenging or unpleasant the task might be. Eating breakfast with him and two other missionaries who lived in our quarters always gave me a boost—not so much because of anything in particular that he said but because of his personal strength and devotion to the work.

Even though I looked forward to breakfast each day, I remember being concerned that Elder Larsen had a slight, barely noticeable tremor in his hand. When he tried to pass a bowl with milk in it one day, the tremor was especially apparent. I asked him what it was, and he shook his head saying, "Not sure, that's just how my hands work."

Following the mission he married, finished undergraduate school, and then went on to complete a doctoral degree at a prestigious university. By the time he had completed the degree, the tremor was worse, and we learned that he had multiple sclerosis. As a missionary he had been so physically alive and active that it was difficult to witness the ravages of MS on his body. At a relatively young age he needed a wheelchair to get around, and eventually he could not be employed full-time. Through it all, he and his wife had a large family of faithful children.

Multiple sclerosis takes a toll not only on the body but also on the emotions, and Elder Larsen was not immune to those effects. But the way his wife cared for him demonstrated the enduring power of a covenant relationship. Even in the darkest moments—and degenerative disease always brings some dark moments—there she was, holding things together, never losing faith, never giving up. The Larsens had been sealed together for eternity, and no disease was going to change that fact. No challenge, whether financial, personal, or medical, could break that covenant attachment they had formed.

I visited Elder Larsen not long before he died. During those final months he was confined to bed, had difficulty talking, and depended on his wife for almost every need. When I greeted him, he immediately recognized me, smiled widely as he always had, and grasped my hand. He and his wife had been married nearly fifty years. They had made much more than a promise or a commitment to each other—they had covenanted with each other and the Lord to cleave together forever.

The marriage covenant contributes to fulfillment of the Abrahamic covenant—that all the world would be blessed by Abraham's seed. Marriage makes it possible for us to have offspring who can one day spread the gospel as missionaries and then also marry and have additional offspring who can do the same. As members of the Church we are children of the covenant—the literal results and beneficiaries of the restoration of the keys of the gathering and the multiplication of Abraham's seed. The covenants we make in mortality build upon that original

Abrahamic covenant, and as we keep the covenants we contribute to all the blessings that the Lord has promised His chosen people.

What stronger bond could there be between God and His children than the covenants we make with Him and that He made with father Abraham? Nothing conveys His love for us more strongly than these covenants, the very blessings that He has covenanted that we will receive. What more could He possibly give us than eternal life—all that the Father hath? The more eager we are to make and keep the covenants He has given us, the stronger our attachment will be our attachment to both the Father and the Son.

On the surface, covenants may appear to be the same for everyone. The Lord sets the terms, and we accept those terms. The terms are identical for everyone. Obedience is obedience and chastity is chastity. But while the terms are the same, our life circumstances affect our efforts to comply with those terms. Covenants draw upon our agency more than any other act in mortality. They are doubly agentic: We choose whether or not we will make them in the first place, and then we choose again whether we will keep them. Elder Larsen and his wife chose to make sacred covenants when they were sealed together, but neither one knew the path that lay ahead for them. To remain married and faithful to each other was qualitatively different for them than for a couple who was not required to endure life-long debilitating illness. Couples living with MS have a much higher rate of divorce than those in the general population.[3]

Elder Larsen and his wife had their own unique path, their own challenges, their own successes. And so do we all. It is true

---

3. CCH Pfleger, EM Flachs, and Nils Koch-Henriksen, "Social consequences of multiple sclerosis. Part 2. Divorce and separation; a historical prospective cohort study," *Multiple Sclerosis Journal*, March 18, 2010, https://journals.sagepub.com/doi/abs/10.1177/1352458510370978?casa_token=2s-s1UIQXfOsAAAAA%3Af7b9KGAuDporM7JQbPH8fgun0Qz6RwTY-qEtiruELbUaan7ZHWvmUJyhsiJ5mTGRuq0fInDO9j9uF&

that the conditions of the covenant are similar for all, but the life circumstances each person faces in mortality can differ dramatically. A good friend of mine has dealt with same-sex attraction throughout his life. He filled a faithful mission and remains faithful today but does not plan to marry in this life. I also have friends, both women and men, who long to marry but have not been able to find a mate. For these friends the marriage covenant has not yet seemed possible, but they continue to faithfully worship in the temple and look forward to the time, perhaps after this life, when they will be able to be sealed to an eternal companion.

When Jesus asked the rich man to sell all of his possessions, Jesus knew that his request would be different for that person than it would be for someone who had no possessions (see Mark 10:21). The covenant to obey or to sacrifice is unique for each individual. Giving up his possessions was too difficult for the rich young man, so he turned away from the Savior, even though Jesus loved him and wanted him to come close and remain faithful. The person with an addiction to drugs or to sex has more difficulty with the covenants of obedience and sacrifice than those without such addictions. No two paths through mortality are the same.

I once had a troubling interview with a young man who had committed a serious transgression. At a tense moment in the interview I said, "So let me see if I understand. What you told me in our last interview was not true, right?" He nodded his head in agreement. Then I said, "I want to know if you feel that you know when you're telling the truth and when you are lying." He looked up and responded, "I'm not sure." I could discern that he was not saying that simply to get sympathy from me. He actually had a problem knowing whether or not he was telling the truth. Some would say that he had a disorder called pathological or compulsive lying. Therefore, the commandment "thou shalt not bear false witness" was different for him than for someone without his mental disorder.

I could give detailed examples for each of the commandments and for each of the covenants we make in the temple, showing how we encounter different paths and different challenges in keeping these commitments. The Lord knew this because the Lord knows our challenges. He knows us each as an individual. He knew when covenants were made that some would face the problems of long-term illness. He knew that some would succumb to addictions and that others would have emotional problems. He knew that the commandments He gave us and the conditions of the covenants He set for us would test us all in unique ways. But that is precisely why He gave us the greatest gifts of all—our agency and His grace so that we can act with faith, obey each commandment, and keep every covenant.

Making and keeping covenants not only strengthens our attachment to God but to others as well. The temple helps us see that covenants bring unity. When we perform ordinances in the temple, individual differences are minimized and collective commitments bring us together as one in Christ. We make covenants in the presence of others who have made those same covenants. Racism, sexism, and ageism disappear as we look upon each other as children of the covenant, children of God. In the temple we sense eternity. We are no longer separated by individual differences but united in our commitment to remain true to the covenants we have made and attached to the one who gave us life.

To strengthen our attachment to God, we need to ponder the meaning of what it means to be a child of the covenant, to be chosen by God to follow Him, to love Him and serve Him. As we permit these sacred covenants to draw us closer to Him, we will feel His presence more in our life. We will know what we must do to fully keep the covenants we have made. We will be filled with His love.

Part Three

STRENGTHENING ATTACHMENTS

T o be filled with the Lord's love is a lifelong endeavor, but perhaps no other purpose should supersede it. Everyone could benefit from receiving more love—every child, every young person, every adult. And everyone could benefit from expressing more love to others. Attachments are the center of our being. They determine our happiness in the here and now, as well as in the hereafter, more than anything else. When our attachment to God is stable, undeviating, and devoted, we feel peace, assurance, and hope. And when our attachment to others is harmonious, enriching, and whole, we feel happiness, wholeness, and calm. Attachments enliven the soul—both body and spirit. They can lift us up when we feel down and renew us when we feel abandoned. So the question looms: can we actually change our attachment style, or are we permanently limited by the attachment patterns we formed as children and youth?

To answer this question, researchers conducted a series of three longitudinal studies with more than 4,000 participants to determine if people who had anxious or avoidant attachment styles could modify their style by exercising their own personal agency. They called it "volitional change"—change that came about because the person *wanted* to change their way of relating to others, and that inner desire caused them to actively work to become less anxious or avoidant. What did the researchers discover? Yes, people can change their patterns of attachment. If they want to become less anxious or less avoidant, they can succeed, but it requires conscious and consistent effort on their part.[1]

This section of the book focuses on how one can change a personal pattern of attachment, not only in relationships with others (as in the study I just recounted) but also in one's relationship

---

1.   Nathan W. Hudson, William J. Chopik, and Daniel A. Briley, "Volitional Change in Adult Attachment: Can People Who Want to Become Less Anxious and Avoidant Move Closer Towards Realizing Those Goals?" *European Journal of Personality 34*, 2019, https://onlinelibrary.wiley.com/doi/full/10.1002/per.2226

with God. Regardless of the quality of one's current relationships, everyone can improve. Some may struggle with anxious patterns, others with avoidant patterns. Some may feel that their current attachment style is healthy and stable. But I believe that most would agree that we can all strengthen our relationships in ways that lead to greater happiness in our own life and in the lives of those we love. Pathways to such change will be different for every individual. The suggestions described in this section of the book are offered to help one find that pathway to change.

BE STILL

Be still and know that I am God.

—D&C 101:16

Seeking stillness in our lives can help us move away from either an anxious or avoidant attachment style. Stillness brings peace. It also can lead to greater trust in others and in God. Stillness comes when faith replaces fear, when oneness replaces loneliness, when we feel safe and secure. Those with an anxious attachment style may shy away from stillness because they feel unworthy or fearful of inevitable self-awareness that accompanies stillness. Others with an avoidant style may not feel they need a sense of stillness in their lives because they feel confident without it. The quality of stillness is difficult to define, but when we see it and experience it, we begin to know what it is.

Although I did not have a name for it then, I observed stillness in an older couple one Sunday in Papeete, Tahiti. I was nineteen years old, had been serving my mission for only a few months, and was trying to get used to the culture, the language, and the humidity. When my companion and I arrived at sacrament meeting, we were asked to help pass the sacrament, something I had not done for several years. I was glad to accept the assignment, but I did not realize at that moment how much that seemingly simple act might affect me.

The week before, a newly baptized middle-aged couple had arrived from Paris. I had met them in the mission home just after their arrival. I remember being surprised at their commanding presence. The husband was a dark-haired, imposing figure befitting his former position in the *gendarmerie* (police force) in France. His wife also had a strong personality, although she had a slight build and was much shorter than her husband. She spoke French faster than anyone I had encountered, and since I was just beginning to learn the language, I found her quite intimidating. They both seemed so confident, so directed, so French.

As I was passing the sacrament on that typically warm Sunday, I came to the edge of the row where this newly arrived couple was seated. I held the bread tray in front of the husband, who was seated by the aisle. He took a piece and held it close to his lips for a few seconds before placing it in his mouth. Then he held the tray for his wife. When he began looking forward again after passing the tray to his wife, I could not help but notice that tears were streaming down both of their faces. A few minutes later when I held the water tray in front of him so he could take the cup, the same thing happened—a noticeable pause as he drew the cup to his lips, and then more tears.

I had actually never seen anyone respond so emotionally to the ordinance of the sacrament. I wondered what had caused them to be so moved as they participated in that ordinance, so I asked my mission president, who knew them well. He responded, "Well, they had to wait years to be baptized because of the husband's position in the *gendarmerie*. You see, the French government viewed our church as a cult and would not allow him to join, so he had to wait until he found new employment here in Tahiti."

I thought about the trials they had obviously encountered in Paris—the pain they had experienced by being forced to wait to join the Church—and then rehearsed in my own mind their reaction as they partook of the sacrament. Not only were they weeping, but they were perfectly still, totally focused on the meaning of the ordinance. I had never had to sacrifice as they had. I had never felt their pain. The sacrament had always been part of my Sunday worship, and so I began to get a glimpse of what I needed to do to make the ordinance more meaningful in my own life.

We usually consider the ordinance of the sacrament as a very personal ritual, a time when we take stock of our life and see where we need to improve. But like all commandments, laws, and ordinances of the gospel, the sacrament has public as well as private implications. In fact, all of our private decisions have public implications. "There is no such thing as private sin."[1]

While teaching a religion course to young adults, my wife and I used a polling app to ask students to rank their most challenging temptations. In every section of the course, the results were the same. Excessive use of social media was more challenging for them than any other kind of temptation. When most of us use social media, we see it as a private thing. "I can use my time how I see fit. I can view what I want to view on my phone. It's my time." But every private action has public implications—the parent who is looking at a phone rather than listening to a child in need, the spouse who is on the phone when the couple needs to communicate, those who view pornography thinking that it is damaging to no one but themselves.

I once attended a priesthood meeting taught by an eighty-year-old man. The lesson was on repentance, and looking a little ashamed the elderly brother said, "My wife tells me that I spend too much time playing video games. Brethren, I need to repent." Quorum members were a bit surprised that video games were as challenging for this senior member of the quorum as they were for children and youth. So many actions that we view as strictly private decisions affect those around us.

---

1. Dean L. Larsen, "A Royal Generation," *Ensign*, May 1983.

The COVID-19 pandemic is a case in point. Some may feel that it is their own private decision whether to follow safety precautions regarding the virus, but the only way the disease can be spread is for one person to pass it to another. The one who makes the "private" decision not to wear a face covering or not to be vaccinated can unintentionally spread the disease to someone else. Private decision—public consequence. The pandemic has taught us the ultimate importance of private decisions.

Because every decision we make affects others, all of our actions affect the quality of our attachments. Even our thoughts affect our relationships. The updated temple recommend questions make this quite clear. For example, one of the questions is, "Do you strive for moral cleanliness in your thoughts and behavior?"[2] How we think about God and others has profound effects on how we relate to them. If we're thinking about the love we have for God or for another, we will act differently toward them than if we feel neglected or forgotten by them.

The stillness we can attain during the sacrament—the kind of stillness I witnessed in the French couple—can lead us to change our thoughts and our behavior. And every such positive change will lead us to greater obedience to the commandments and stronger commitment to keeping our covenants. Because every commandment and covenant is intended to strengthen our relationship to God and to others, the sacrament, then, becomes an ordinance focused on attachments. During the ordinance I might ask myself, "How can I draw nearer to the Lord, and how can I show more love to those around me?"

Actively seeking more stillness in our lives can lead to significant improvements in our relationships. Such stillness can happen during daily prayer, in silent meditation, or at any time

2. The Church of Jesus Christ of Latter-say Saints, "Church Updates Temple Recommend Interview Questions," *Newsroom*, October 2019, https://newsroom.churchofjesuschrist.org/article/october-2019-general-conference-temple-recommend

we can detach ourselves from the distractions that surround us. This is not easy in a culture that is saturated with diversions, but it is worth every effort we can devote to it. In these quiet moments we can focus on the love we have for the Lord and for others. If we are still enough, we can feel love for Heavenly Parents, the Savior, and others. We can be inspired to know how we might strengthen our attachment to the Divine, as well as to our neighbor. In these quiet moments, we hear the Lord say, "Be still and know that I am God."

Invitations:

Welcome stillness.
Replace fear with stillness.
Be still and be one with God and with others.
Let distractions go and stillness will come.

MAKE YOUR EMOTION

See that ye bridle all your passions,
that ye may be filled with love.

—Alma 38:12

While serving as a stake president, I went to the dry cleaner to pick up a suit I had dropped off the week before. I gave the young attendant my name, and then I waited for an unusually long time. She finally returned and with a sheepish grin on her face said, "I can't find your suit." I responded, "You mean it isn't done yet?" She said, "No, I mean we can't find any record of you dropping it off." I gave her the claim check, and she then became even more embarrassed. "I'm sure you dropped it off, but somehow it's been lost," she responded. At that point I wasn't sure what I said, but it was likely neither kind nor understanding. After I drove away, I began thinking to myself, "She's probably a member of my stake and will no longer have any respect for me."

I could not help but contrast my reaction at the dry cleaner with the response I had seen recently between an airline agent and a customer. My flight had been canceled, and I was waiting in line to get rebooked. The woman in front of me began yelling at the agent, "But I have to be in Australia tomorrow! I have to!" In an understanding and completely calm tone, the agent replied, "I know you were planning to be in Australia tomorrow morning, but there is no other flight to Sydney at this time of day—not on our airline or on any other airline. There's just no way to get you there. I'm sorry." He then went on to explain what the airline could do for her to compensate for the cancelled flight, but she would not be consoled. She kept yelling at him, and he kept being patient and kind with her.

I wondered why I had not been as patient with the young woman at the dry cleaner as the flight agent had been with the irate customer. I had allowed the lost suit to cause me to lose patience, just as the woman trying to get to Australia had allowed the cancelled flight to push her anger button. When unexpected problematic things happen, are we at the mercy of our emotions? Is anger or impatience or hurt or discouragement unavoidable? How much control do we have over the way we feel at an upsetting moment?

It is tempting to conclude that emotions just happen to us—that they are beyond our control. The parent who loses his or her temper regularly would like to think that there is no other way to react to children's misbehavior, that it's the situation itself that causes the emotion, not the person experiencing the emotion. We sometimes want to think that all emotions are like the fight-or-flight response that occurs when a rattlesnake slithers across our hiking path. But if that's the case, then why do the scriptures teach us to "bridle all our passions" and to restrain angry thoughts and behavior? (see Alma 38:12; 3 Nephi 12:22).

It would be nice if we did not need to take responsibility for our emotions, if we could simply blame our foul mood or outburst or harsh word on someone or something else. But that would mean we would be "acted upon"—that we would cease to act on our own agency (see 2 Nephi 2:14). Not even those who study the brain and analyze emotions will let us rationalize. After years of research on emotions, a neuroscientist affirmed that we make our own emotions; we cannot blame them on outside forces. Lisa Feldman Barret said, "Emotions are not temporary deviations from rationality. They are not alien forces that invade you without your consent. They are not tsunamis that leave destruction in their wake. They are not even your reactions to the world. They are your constructions of the world. Instances of emotion are no more out of control than thoughts or perceptions or beliefs or memories."[1]

We may like to think that our emotions are somehow separate and distinct from our thoughts and that we can gain more control of our thoughts than we can of our emotions. Arthur Henry King, a Latter-day Saint, British educator, poet, and philosopher, once said to me in the middle of a conversation, "Remember, there is no thought without emotion, and no emotion without thought." He went on to explain that people often try to separate the "heart and the mind"—the heart being the seat of emotion, and the mind being the seat of logical thought. Then he concluded, "There's only one problem with that idea, a person is one united whole—you cannot separate a person in two pieces: a thought piece and an emotion piece."[2]

Brother King made a point much like that of the neuroscientist. Thoughts and emotions are intertwined and cannot be separated. Thoughts can lead to emotions, and emotions can lead to other thoughts. Our task in mortality is to recognize the relationship between our thoughts and emotions and gain control of both. The new temple recommend questions help us understand the importance of striving to gain control of our thoughts as well as our actions. Harsh words can hurt any relationship. A child who feels unappreciated—or worse yet, abused—by a parent has difficulty forming a secure attachment to the parent. A spouse who feels forgotten has difficulty cleaving to the one she married. Siblings and friends who regularly berate or verbally attack each other weaken the bond between them.

Those with an avoidant attachment style may have difficulty controlling their anger. They may blame others for their emotional reactions rather than intentionally exercising constraint. Those with

---

1. Lisa Feldman Barrett, *How Emotions are Made: The Secret Life of the Brain* (Boston: Houghton Mifflin Harcourt, 2017).
2. Personal communication, 1994.

an anxious style are often overcome by fear to the point that they become dysfunctional. How can those with attachment difficulties of any type modify their emotional response? One possible solution comes from neuroscientists who describe how to change our emotional response in a particular situation.[3] They call it "switching sets." These "sets" are the situations we encounter, the context in which two people relate to each other. One set may be two young adults beginning a dating relationship, while another set might be the family relationships that each one experienced while growing up. Those with avoidant or anxious styles developed certain ways of behaving so that they could cope with parental rejection or neglect. But when they use those same behaviors with someone who is *not* rejecting them, they damage the relationship they are trying to strengthen. So the answer is to recognize that the situation has changed, and that the overlearned behaviors one developed as a child or youth are no longer appropriate in the new situation.

To strengthen attachments we need to learn how to "switch sets," to give up old ways of relating and adopt new ones. Scientists refer to this type of change as "volitional."[4] Volition is simply "willing" the change. Such change means we need to draw upon the gift of agency that God gave us and choose to replace harshness with praise, impatience with long-suffering, dissatisfaction with love. We can choose to see the momentary lapses in those around us as just that, momentary. We need to recognize that we are all on the pathway to perfection, that no one will be perfect in this life. We can make allowance for our own emotional missteps, just as we can for the missteps of others.

---

3. Hal Shorey, "Attachment Styles and the Art of Self-Control," *Psychology Today*, 2020, https://www.psychologytoday.com/us/blog/the-freedom-change/202011/attachment-styles-and-the-art-self-control.
4. Nathan W. Hudson, William J. Chopik, and Daniel A. Briley, "Volitional Change in: Can People Who Want to Become Less Anxious and Avoidant Move Closer Toward Realizing Those Goals?" *The Journal of Analytical Psychology 34*, 2019, https://onlinelibrary.wiley.com/doi/full/10.1002/per.2226.

Anger, of course, is not the only emotion we must learn to regulate. Sadness, grief, and even elation are also feelings that we must recognize and deal with. A person can be overly jocular, laughing inappropriately at a comment that was meant to be serious. Empathy demands that we feel as another feels, and that means sensing the moments when we need to feel a person's pain rather than trying to laugh it away. Likewise, we need to mourn with those that mourn. Grief is a very real, necessary emotion that sweeps over us and seems to overwhelm us. Grief's grip can be tight and unyielding. It often persists much longer than we would like. But it can also be a healing emotion that can help us move forward after losing someone we love. I remember a funeral I attended in which President Gordon B. Hinckley spoke directly to the family members of the deceased, helping them understand how necessary it is to grieve. Grief is often not limited to sadness. It can include feelings of guilt, anger, and regret. Working through these emotions following the loss of a loved one is essential for our own emotional well-being.

We cannot turn ourselves over to an emotion that could eventually paralyze us or do damage to others. Whether we are dealing with anger, sadness, discouragement, grief, or some form of hyper-insensitivity, we need to take a step back, remember that we have been given the divine gift of agency, and do whatever it takes to bring our emotions within our control rather than yielding control to any outside force. We need to give up the old way of reacting and trade it in for a new, healthier way. We may need to seek help from loved ones, friends, or professionals when needed, always remembering that we are ultimately in control of how we feel and how we react to others, how we show love, and how we give counsel and correction.

Invitations:

Choose to make your own emotions.
Choose to make your own thoughts.
Embrace new and healthier ways of reacting to others.
Pray for emotional control.
Give your whole soul to Him.

USE CANDOR
WITH KINDNESS

*I did frankly forgive them
all that they had done.*

—1 Nephi 7:21

Those who have an avoidant attachment style usually speak their mind with ease, often with bluntness and sometimes even with cruelty. They are typically not concerned about how the other person will react, because relationships are not important to them. They feel adequately self-assured in their own right. In contrast, the one who has an anxious attachment style is fearful of damaging or even losing a relationship, so they might speak with kindness at the expense of expressing how they actually feel. *Candor* means clarity and brightness or truthfulness. *Kindness* infers that one speaks with care for the other person. Those with an avoidant style often focus too much on clarity, "saying it like it is," while those with an anxious style emphasize kindness without speaking truthfully. In neither case does the person strengthen an attachment with the other person. Those with a healthy, secure attachment use both candor and kindness, and the more such communication flows between two people, the stronger and healthier the attachment will become.

The scene is familiar in families: one sibling tries to help his other siblings by correcting them, but the two receiving correction are offended, get angry, and attack the one trying to help them. Usually the anger leads to verbal attacks, but in the case of Nephi correcting Laman and Lemuel, they actually tried to kill him by tying him up and leaving him alone to die. After he prayed for strength and the bands were loosed, what did Nephi do? Did he retaliate? No, he "frankly" forgave them (1 Nephi 7:21).

Nephi was in control of his emotions, but his brothers were not. They let their feelings of offense escalate into anger, so much so that they wanted to take Nephi's life. When my wife and I were raising our children we would often quote King Benjamin, who counseled his people not to "fight and quarrel one with another" (Mosiah 4:14). Fighting emanates from feelings of anger, so again we learn that bridling our passions is essential if we are to develop lasting, healthy, secure attachments to those we have been given to love.

Nephi went beyond merely forgiving his brothers for attempting to take his life; he frankly forgave them. Frankness sometimes connotes harshness, but that is not the meaning of the word. When we speak frankly, we communicate with openness, honesty, and directness, especially in unpalatable situations. Nephi's situation was more than unpalatable. He could have returned to his brethren and lashed out at them for trying to kill him. He could have gone back to them sulking, showing how much they had hurt his feelings, as well as the skin on his arms that had been injured by the ropes. But he didn't. He confronted them kindly without any feelings of vengeance and openly and honestly forgave them. He forgave them with candor.

While serving as mission president I received a call from a missionary who was about to be visited by his zone leaders to receive additional training. "I don't want them to come. They don't need to come. We're doing okay," he said as if he was issuing an order. I responded, "They are not coming to attack you. They're coming to help in any way you want them to. They visit every companionship, and it's your turn. I hope you will accept their help." The missionary paused and mumbled something I could not understand, but I could tell he still did not want them to come.

The missionary was feeling offended even at the thought of receiving correction. He may have been afraid that the zone leaders might see something in his district that they didn't approve of. I'm not sure. But his reaction was defensive even before he had anything to be defensive about. Following the visit I called the missionary and asked him how things went. He said, "Okay, they were actually pretty helpful. I don't know why I was so worried. They really helped us out a lot."

The zone leaders taught with both candor and kindness. If they saw something that needed correction, they did not shy away from it but showed the companionship how they might improve—all in kindness, in a spirit of wanting to help them. Nephi was trying to do the same as he corrected Laman and Lemuel. But they took offense and attacked him.

Elder Neal A. Maxwell once counseled: "Be grateful for people in your lives who love you enough to correct you. . . . Correction can be an act of affection."[1] Candor sometimes connotes correction, but when that correction is given with kindness, the one being corrected can feel the love that accompanies it. Thus, the missionaries who were mentored by the zone leaders found, to their surprise, that they felt better after the visit than they had before, sensing that the correction would actually help them and that it was coming to them out of love, not from a desire to punish them.

Communication in families requires candor and kindness. Correction requires affection. We speak with openness, honesty, and frankness, infused with kindness, never with rancor. Never disparaging or belittling another. Never in retaliation. Always in simple, honest, open, and uplifting communication. We seek to give correction in our families as the Lord gives correction: "For whom the Lord loveth he correcteth; even as a father the son in whom he delighteth" (Proverbs 3:12).

I believe Laman and Lemuel repented so quickly after Nephi "frankly" forgave them because Nephi's forgiving words came from his heart. They could feel that Nephi still loved them even though they knew he should not have felt that way after what they

---

1.   Neal A. Maxwell, "Remember How Merciful the Lord Hath Been," *Ensign*, May 2004.

had done to him. They should have asked him to forgive them, but Nephi was the first to express forgiveness and love. He knew that the attachment to his two brothers, although they were resistant, was more important than anything else, especially more important than the emotional and physical pain his brothers had caused him.

The original meaning of the word *candor* was brightness, whiteness, or purity. So, when the Lord characterizes charity as the pure love of Christ, he is reminding us that His love comes with brightness, openness, and honesty. The Lord loves with candor and kindness, always to lift, help, and succor us. We need love like this in all our close relationships—with God and with others.

Nephi so movingly forgave his brethren because his heart was filled with the Lord's pure love. He forgave them as the Savior forgives us, even when we may not deserve forgiveness, even when we are down on ourselves and feel like giving up. Jesus always forgave with candor and kindness, whether He was speaking with the repentant sinner or to those who were seeking to entrap Him with foolishness. Even on the cross, He asked His Father with openness, honesty, and frankness to forgive the ones who had driven the nails through His flesh, because even in His final moments, He was filled with divine love.

Whatever our attachment style might be, we can increase our capacity to love the way the Savior loves us by being honest, open, and frank in our communications with each other. This kind of communication means that we do not hide from challenging issues that confront us. We do not pretend that all is well when all is not well. We admit our wrongs, forgive, and look for ways to lift each other. Like the zone leaders who went to help their fellow missionaries, we ask where help is needed so we can face problems together.

Invitations:

> *Be open.*
> *Be honest.*
> *Use candor.*
> *And always be kind.*

IMMERSE
YOURSELF
IN LIFE

I feel my Savior's love in all the world around me.
His Spirit warms my soul through everything I see.

—K. Newell Dayley

The sound of a mountain stream against the rocks of a creek bed. The sunlight filtering through the aspens, maples, and pines. The hum of a dragonfly. The soothing flight of a butterfly as it navigates on motionless wings. The breathtaking steep rise of the mountains on both sides of a trail. At these moments I feel surrounded with life: trees and other plants are alive, creatures are in motion, water is the source of life, mountains provide stability. The Japanese call these experiences *shinrin-yoku*: *shinrin* meaning "forest," and *yoku* meaning "to bathe." So, in English we might say forest bathing. In the gospel sense it's the moment when you see beyond your own being, when you recognize that everything around you came from a God who loves you—the one who created all life, all out of love. Forest bathing, then, can be a way to strengthen our attachment to the one who gave us life, not only life on earth but life eternal.

Robert Louis Stevenson once described the forest as a place where one can find spiritual renewal: "It is not so much for its beauty that the forest makes a claim upon [our] hearts, as for that subtle something, that quality of air that emanates from old trees, that so wonderfully changes and renews a weary spirit."[1] Spiritual renewal is all about attachment—attachment to God through His creations and attachment to others. Being alone in the forest has a special peace-giving power to it, but being with someone else in the forest allows you to share the beauty together, renewing each other's spirits.

One does not need to be in the mountains, as I was when I wrote that first paragraph. Forest bathing can happen in a large city. I once sat on a park bench in the Jardin du Luxembourg in Paris, France. The massive, geometrically configured bed of carefully groomed flowers sprawled out in front of me, but what caught my eye was a mother, her son, and a bird high in a tree above them. The young boy pointed to the bird and exclaimed, "Look, Mom, that bird's going into its nest!" The mother immediately connected to her son, looked up at the bird, and said with astonishment, "I've never seen a bird like that, and I've never seen one go into its nest!" She was as excited about the bird as was her son. The mother and her child were attached by their enthusiasm for a bird entering its nest.

During the creation scene in an endowment session my wife and I attended, an actual live bat flew across the room in front of the screen. At first, we wondered if something about the image on the screen might have given the impression of a bat. But when the bat flew back across the screen before it disappeared, we knew it was real. Some perhaps felt that the bat detracted from the sacredness of the moment, but I saw it differently. I saw the bat as a very tangible, visible reminder that God created all living things because God loved us enough to provide us with the necessities to sustain our own lives, but also with natural beauty that is beyond description to sustain our souls. He did this all out of love. All because of His attachment to us, which is "fixed and immovable," the very kind of relationship that He knows we can form with each other in our family and circle of friends (see D&C 88:133).

---

1. Hannah Fries, *Forest Bathing Retreat* (North Adams, MA: Storey Publishing, 2018), 1.

To form healthy attachments one must be fully present. It is in the quiet moments—moments when we are away from devices, tasks, and pressures—that we can feel at one with ourselves and with God. Being fully present in the moment means listening with openness and understanding, being patient in communication rather than hastily jumping to conclusions, letting the other person in, and allowing an unexpected comment or nonverbal response to help us see things we've never seen before or to understand old things in a new way.

When we immerse ourselves in life we feel safe and secure. We cherish beauty. The life of other living things, especially the life of another person, can bring us to a living God, One who cares for us, sustains us, and nurtures us with unending love. Those who detach themselves from life and focus on objects—the things that distract us and move us away from others—feel anxious about their own life and about their future. The powerful antidote for anxiety is love— the kind of love that the Savior has for us and that we can have for others, reminding us who we really are, and bringing us back to life.

Immersing ourselves in life reminds us that all life is sacred, that every person is sacred and that life was created by a God who is filled with love for all of us, a God who wants us to be filled with love for Him and for His children. So the next time you are close to nature in a forest or a park, an ocean, a desert, or a stream, let all the living things around you bring you home to yourself. Let the warmth of life—the living beauty of all God's creations—bring reassurance to your soul that God is with you, that He is aware of your needs as well as your gifts, that He was attached to you before this world was created, and He will continue to be attached to you forever.

Invitations:

Surround yourself with life.
See beyond your own being.
Sense God's love in His creations.
Share the beauty of living things with others.

SEE AS GOD SEES

We act on our perceptions of reality, not on reality itself.

Think of the stark contrast between Alma's perception of Abinadi and King Noah's priests' perception of Abinadi. Alma saw him as a prophet, while the other priests viewed him as an enemy of the people (see Mosiah 17). Consider the similar disparity between how Sam and Nephi viewed their father with the perceptions of Laman and Lemuel (see 1 Nephi). Concerning both of these prophets, perceptions were at the root of the relationship. Alma revered Abinadi; the other priests hated him. Sam and Nephi loved their father and followed him. Laman and Lemuel dismissed their father as deluded and foolish (see 1 Nephi 2:11). How do people perceive another person in such dramatically different ways? This question lies at the heart of how we form attachments with one another and with God.

When I was a teenager my friend's sister returned home from the university she attended and told her father that a young man had proposed marriage to her and that she was troubled about it. The father asked her to recount the experience. She responded, "Well, he and I were sitting on a ledge around a flower bed on campus, and all of a sudden, he looked at me and said, 'God told me last night that I should marry you!' Dad, I didn't know what to say without hurting him, because I don't feel the same. He totally blindsided me." The father then counseled her not to worry about the encounter but to contact the young man and tell him that she did not feel the same as he did, and that she was not planning to marry him.

The young man misperceived how the young woman felt about him. Those approaching marriage must be equally in love with and committed to each other. Their perceptions must align. Perceptions can either clarify or cloud the nature of any attachment, and it is perceptions that drive our actions, not reality itself. If I perceive that God loves me, which is the actual reality, I will act in ways that will bring me closer to him and to His children. If I perceive that He does not love me, which is an incorrect view of reality, I will distance myself from Him and from others.

One author has explained that perception is akin to painting: "Perception is like painting a scenery—no matter how beautifully you paint, it will still be a painting of the scenery, not the scenery itself."[1] And why is the painting never quite like the scenery itself? Because the painting—the way we see things—is influenced by how we see ourselves, how we see others, and how we interpret every experience we have ever had.

Nephi asked that he might have the same visionary experience as his father, and that vision helped to cement his faith in his father as a prophet. Laman and Lemuel did not seek such an experience, and so their perception of their father was different from Nephi's. When Abinadi was preaching to King Noah, Alma opened himself to the Spirit, while the other priests did not. Their wickedness clouded their view.

Captain Moroni was a man of God, but he completely misperceived Pahoran's lack of response to his request for provisions and reinforcements, assuming that Pahoran did not care about supporting his troops (see Alma 60). Even the respected leader Moroni had an inaccurate perception. The picture Moroni first

---

1.   Abhijit Naskar, *Human Making Is Our Mission: A Treatise on Parenting* (Google Books, 2017),, https://books.google.com/books/about/Human_Making_is_Our_Mission.html?id=lzlJDwAAQBAJ&source=kp_book_descriptionf

painted was inaccurate. The woman at the well initially misper-ceived who Jesus was, but she listened—not only listened but opened herself to truth—and became convinced that Jesus was the Christ (see John 4:29). Likewise, Abish, the Lamanite woman, correctly perceived that King Lamoni had been overcome by the Spirit, when everyone else misperceived the situation and thought he had died. The Pharisees who were with Jesus never saw Him for who He really was.

All of these cases show why the scriptures repeatedly caution that some have eyes but do not see, and ears but do not hear. Even His disciples misperceived what had happened when Jesus fed the four thousand: "Why reason ye, because ye have no bread? perceive ye not yet, neither understand? have ye your heart yet hardened? *Having eyes, see ye not? and having ears, hear ye not?*" (Mark 8:17–18; italics added). The scriptures repeatedly warn us against these inadequate perceptions.

In all of our relationships perception is at the root. Moroni's misperception of Paharon's actions temporarily strained their relationship. The relationship between Jesus and the woman at the well was transformed as soon as she recognized Him as the Savior. Perception drives our actions, and actions either strengthen or weaken our attachments. Even in everyday commu-nication perception is key. If my wife asks me to do something, I might see her request as a helpful reminder or as an attack on my thoughtlessness. When a friend fails to respond to an invita-tion, the potential recipient might see the non-response as a snub, while the friend may have simply forgotten to respond or failed to receive the invitation all together.

If we want to be filled with the Lord's love, we need to con-stantly be aware of our own perceptions. The person with an anx-ious attachment style often has a clouded perception of the other person's feelings. As described earlier in the diagram illustrating attachments, if the anxious person doesn't receive a response to a text, it is interpreted that the person doesn't like them anymore, when the person may simply not have taken the time to respond as quickly as the other desired. Those with avoidant styles may constantly be looking for reasons to distrust the other person, so every shortcoming in the other is seen as evidence that they should avoid trusting the person.

Perception underlies our communication style and our reactions to others' communication styles—the way we see ourselves and the way we see others. The only way we can paint a more accurate picture of the scenery around us is to rely on divine help. The Lord can help us discern our misperceptions. He can help us see things as they really are, as Jacob taught: "The Spirit speaketh the truth and lieth not. Wherefore, it speaketh of things as they really are, and of things as they really will be; wherefore, these things are manifested unto us plainly, for the salvation of our souls" (Jacob 4:13). Jacob was helping his people understand that God does not misperceive. The scene God paints matches reality in every detail. He sees into each person's heart, not misjudging by outward appearances. He sees the motives behind the actions. If we want to see as God sees, then we must listen to the Spirit, adjust our perceptions, and act on divine inspiration. We must draw on His power to learn to discern so that our relationships with Him and with others will be based on truth and not on lies. As our actions are driven by the Lord, we will be filled with His love.

Invitations:

> *Perceive clearly and truthfully.*
> *Let go of misperceptions.*
> *See others as God sees them.*
> *Avoid interpreting the motives of others.*

ENGAGE IN GOOD CONVERSATION

Let him shew out of a good conversation
his works with meekness of wisdom.

—James 3:13

My wife and I have close friends we met in the early years of our marriage, and we have remained close throughout our lives. We find ways to get together periodically even though we do not live in the same city. While driving home following each of these visits, we have the same feeling that is difficult for either of us to describe. Our friends always make us feel better—not only better, but uplifted, more faithful, more committed to the Lord. Our conversations with these friends go on for hours, but we never really tire of talking. The topics range from the mundane to the miraculous, from everyday trials, to our deepest hopes and dreams. As I reflect on our time together, I cannot recall a bad conversation in which any of us felt worse for the words that were said. I can recall only good conversations.

If we want to strengthen our attachment to others within our family or without, we need more good conversations, the kind of conversations I've described with our friends. Such conversations are essential within our families. One of the unexpected benefits of the COVID-19 pandemic has been our online chats with our entire family each Sunday afternoon. Using FaceTime or Zoom, we connect with all five children and their families. A different family takes charge of the meeting each week. That family chooses what we will talk about and who will conduct the session. We have always stayed in touch by phone and group text with each of our children, but each Sunday session is more like a short family reunion. Cousins can see and talk to each other. Parents and children can bear testimony. We can all enjoy being together. The conversation is always uplifting. Like visits with our lifelong friends, we always feel better following these conversations.

I believe good conversation is a unique combination of teaching and therapy. The best teachers help learners see lessons that have been inside for a long time but may never have come to consciousness. A great teacher is not a robotic deliverer of information. This teacher understands the needs and gifts of the learner and helps reveal those needs and gifts to the learner. Similarly skilled therapists try to help their clients see things in themselves and others that they haven't been able to see before so that they can begin to act differently. In gospel teaching and gospel-centered therapy the learner is always drawn closer to God.

I have often joked that my wife is my best therapist. But I'm not really joking. She knows me best. She can read me better than anyone else. She knows when I'm down and when I'm feeling well. And she knows how to redirect my thoughts when I need to change the way I'm approaching life at a particular moment. How does she do it? Through conversation. Words are the most powerful tools we have to help each other. Some of these words are expressed in prayer, and others are expressed in conversation. My wife can also be my best teacher. She listens, asks questions for clarification, and then helps me see something in a new and better way.

Some find it easy to converse with others; some do not. As my wife and I have worked with young single adults, we have encouraged them to meet new people so that they can eventually find a marriage partner. We are basically inviting them to have more good conversations with more people. We ask them to talk with a new person until they can find at least one thing they have in common with this individual. I like to demonstrate how easy this is by asking someone in a class or meeting—someone I've never met before—to come to the front and have a conversation with me. I then show the assembled group how easy it is to begin a conversation and find something in common.

Malcolm Gladwell popularized the term *connector* to describe the person who is always trying to get diverse people or diverse ideas together.[1] Connectors are people with a secure attachment style who find it extremely easy, even irresistible, to meet new people and help the ones they meet to connect with others. Once when my wife and I were working out in a gym nearly every day, we met someone who we lovingly called "the connector." He approached me one day and wanted to discuss an idea from a talk I had given. That conversation led to others, and then one day, he said, "I know another person in the gym here that you need to meet." So I went with him and met the man he thought I should meet. As we were approaching this man, my connector friend said, "I know you two will have some things in common." It turned out that we had a lot in common, more than I could have imagined. Because our connector friend knew both of us, he knew we would enjoy getting to know each other.

Opposite on the continuum from the connector might be the person with selective mutism, a disability that causes a person to avoid speaking to anyone at any time. I once interviewed a young man on the first day of his mission and asked if there might be something I should know about him that would help me serve him better. He responded, "Well, I've never talked with anyone before." His response at first caught me off guard. He was speaking to me

---

1. Malcolm Gladwell, *The Tipping Point: How Little Things Can make a Big Difference* (Boston: Little, Brown, and Company, 2000).

right at that moment, so I probed a little further. "You mean you're quiet?" "No," he said, "I mean I never talk to anyone outside my own family unless I absolutely have to." I then asked him how he handled school: "So what happened if a teacher called on you in class?" He explained that teachers knew that he would not respond, so they never called on him. I asked, "So what about friends?" He responded, "I don't have any friends."

Our conversation that day was unsettling for me in a number of ways. I wondered how he had gone through life selectively speaking only to members of his family while inside his own home. I also wondered how he could possibly have gathered the courage to submit his papers and go on a mission. I kept in touch with him often. One day I called and asked, "I want to know how often people ask you why you don't talk more." He said, "All day, every day." Then he expressed the pain he felt at their constant pressure for him to talk. I then said, "I want you to try something. I want you to do two things—that's all, just two things: speak up and speak first." He spoke so quietly that it was hard to hear him when he did speak, so that was the first challenge. I then promised him that if he would speak before his companion spoke, saying anything he wanted to say, people would not see him as such a quiet person.

Time passed. He took my challenges, and the results were greater than we had hoped. He began doing trainings during zone conference, talks in sacrament meeting, and of course daily discourse as a missionary with those who were interested in hearing the message of the restored gospel. Following his mission a member of his ward sought me out to tell me how amazed he was to see the change in this young man. He clearly learned how to have good conversations with everyone he met. He learned something about vulnerability—opening himself to new experiences with people he had never met before.

This young missionary did not need to have the connector personality, and neither do we. However, we might be able to benefit from emulating some of the connector characteristics. We need to be more vulnerable than we typically are. We need to be willing and open to new and unexpected experiences. The missionary could have ignored my suggestions to speak up and speak first, but he didn't. He embraced them, and doing so helped him break through a barrier that he had struggled with all of his life.

In our families we also need to be open and vulnerable. Vulnerability is often seen as a negative emotion, but it is essential in close relationships. Someone with an avoidant attachment style is typically afraid of vulnerability, seeing it as a sign of personal weakness. Those with an anxious style are often afraid to open up to others for fear that others might discover their personal weaknesses. To be vulnerable means that we are willing to take risks in order to draw closer to someone. It does not mean that we take undue risks that could lead to destructive behavior. But it does mean that we need to be willing to share how we really feel, even when those feelings are sensitive and fragile. Otherwise we cannot progress to the next step on our pathway to becoming more like the Savior. Good conversation can lead us forward if we are willing to open ourselves to others and to the Lord. Good conversation will strengthen our attachment to God and to others, and we can help others connect so that they also can strengthen their attachments.

Invitations:

> *We open ourselves and become vulnerable.*
> *We connect.*
> *We help others connect.*
> *All through good conversation.*

FIND A NEW FRIEND

*In everyone's life, at some time, our inner fire
goes out. It is then burst into flame by an
encounter with another human being.
We should all be thankful for those people
who rekindle the inner spirit.*[1]

—Albert Schweitzer

We call them friends, but what does it really mean to be a friend?
We know a friend is much more than the watered-down meaning
of the word on social media. Someone may have 500 "friends"
on Facebook, but how many of those people really know the one
they've friended? It is a sad irony that young adults in the United
States who frequently use social media are twice as likely to experience loneliness as those who seldom use it.[2]

A friend is more than an acquaintance, more than someone
you share time with. A friend knows you—your interests, your
goals, your hopes, and your heartaches. A friend can see things
in you that you may not see in yourself, and that same friend can

---

1. Albert Schweitzer Quotes. (n.d.) BrainyQuote.com. Retrieved August
   28, 2020 from BrainyQuote.com, https://www.brainyquote.com/quotes/
   albert_schweitzer_105225
2. Brian A. Primack et. al. "Social Media Use and Perceived Social Isolation
   Among Young Adults," *U.S. American Journal of Preventative Medicine 53*,
   2017, https://www.ajpmonline.org/article/S0749-3797(17)30016-8/fulltext

help you see the world a little bit differently. Friends see through each other's eyes. They suffer when the other is in pain and rejoice when the other experiences joy. They offer to help without being asked, to grieve with each other, to lift, succor, and nurture each other.

Some friendships happen quite naturally as if they were meant to be, but other friendships form between two people who seemingly have little in common, little that would bring them together. My father forged one of these unlikely unions with a man named Skip Tobata, and the friendship lasted his entire life. Dad worked with Skip in the car business and saw him nearly every day. Skip and his wife, Mary, became friends of our whole family. As I was growing up, I did not realize that their relationship might seem improbable. The relationship taught me much about what it means to love others with different backgrounds and cultural traditions. The story of my father, Wes, and his friend Skip actually begins at the end of Skip's life.

The Protestant minister stepped to the podium following the final speaker and said, "The family has asked that Wes Osguthorpe, a trusted friend of Skip, now place the final rose on the coffin." I turned to Dad and whispered, "Do you want some help?" He said nothing—he spoke only when he needed to—but just shook his head and then began to stand and move to Skip's casket.

Dad had been suffering from Parkinson's disease for over two decades, so his feet did not move as they once did. As he shuffled toward the casket, an unusual hush came over the audience, some perhaps wondering if Dad might fall while others may have been touched by watching my father pay one last tribute to a close friend. Then, with a simple forward movement of his arm, Dad placed the final rose on top of Skip's casket.

Theirs was an unlikely alliance. While in his twenties, Skip and his family—all American citizens—had spent World War II in the Topaz Relocation Center, a euphemistic term for an internment camp for US residents of Japanese descent. *Internment* means "prison." So Skip and his family spent World War II in a US prison in the desert west of Delta, Utah.

While Skip was locked away in the desert, Wes was fighting in Okinawa. Dad never spoke about the war until he was close to the end of his life. Like so many soldiers, he felt it was too gruesome to remember. But in his seventies he would, if asked, recount how he watched his foxhole buddy die right next to him. Although I seldom saw Dad become emotional, he always cried when he retold this story. He also described with similar emotion how he watched a fellow soldier die on the battlefield only a few feet away from his foxhole. He would say, "I kept waiting for the medics to come, but they never did. They just let him die there in the dirt."

The battle of Okinawa lasted eighty-two days, from April to mid-June of 1945. The Normandy beaches of France had already been won. The war was almost over. But the Pacific theater was still raging. And Wes was right in the middle of it. This battle was referred to as the "typhoon of steel" because of the ferocity of the fighting, the intensity of the kamikaze attacks (Japanese suicide bombers), and the sheer size of the fighting force. It was the bloodiest of all battles in the Pacific theater with 14,009 Allied deaths and more than 65,000 casualties of all kinds. Japan lost 77,166 soldiers and 42,000–150,000 civilians.[3]

Wes was wounded in the battle. His back would never be the same. He was flown from Okinawa to a hospital in Seattle for treatment, while his wife and two young daughters waited for him back home in Utah. I have memories as a boy of seven or eight years old, hearing my dad in the middle of the day screaming in pain as he lay on his back in his bedroom. No one seemed to be able to do anything for him when his back pain reemerged. The effects of Okinawa never left him.

---

3. "Battle of Okinawa," Wikipedia, 2020, https://en.m.wikipedia.org/wiki/Battle_of_Okinawa

When Wes returned from the war, he found a job as a mechanic in Salt Lake City with the L.H. Strong Motor Company. I wish I could have been there when Wes met Skip. Skip was also a mechanic at L.H. Strong. I imagine it was a fairly uneventful first encounter. I don't think Dad ever saw Skip as Japanese, and Skip did not see Dad as someone who had been shooting at those of his Japanese heritage. They saw each other as friends. And their friendship never wavered. They were different in so many ways—in appearance, in religion, in ethnic origin—but lifelong friends.

When I was a young boy, we visited the Tobata family, and on the way home from one of these visits Mom, with frustration in her voice, said, "I just don't understand why they can't buy a home. They deserve one as much as anyone else." During our visit, Skip and Mary had described without any rancor how they were renting because those of Japanese descent were not allowed to purchase homes in certain neighborhoods.

Skip could have been full of resentment for the way his family had been imprisoned during the war or even how they were treated following the war. Dad could have developed a hatred of anyone who even resembled those who had wounded him and killed his fellow soldiers in Okinawa. But there were none of those feelings in either one. Our families kept in touch right to the end of their lives.

I was glad I was able to sit next to Dad at Skip's funeral during that final act of love for his friend. Skip, like Wes, suffered from Parkinson's disease. Their symptoms emerged at similar times and progressed along the same hauntingly relentless path. But Dad still had enough muscle control, and he definitely had more than enough will to say a final farewell to a friend.

Friends come into our lives in many ways. As children we make friends who often influence us as we move through youth and then adulthood. These childhood friends are the first attachments we experience beyond our family. They know us in some fundamental ways. They feel our pain when we get hurt and call for help when we need it. They laugh with us and cry with us as we confront so many experiences for the first time.

For the first nine years of my life I lived across the fence from the Hinckleys. I remember President Gordon B. Hinckley as a stake president and later as he received his other callings as a General Authority and prophet. President and Sister Hinckley's son Clark was my closest childhood friend. When we were twelve years old, we went to a picnic in the park close to our homes. As we were preparing to eat, Sister Hinckley asked Clark to go to their car and get the cooler with the food.

As Clark and I were approaching their VW Beetle, I said, "I know how to drive that car." Clark didn't know it, but my father had allowed me to learn how to drive when I was twelve, so he said, "You do not!" I responded, "Give me the keys." So I got in the driver's seat, and he sat in the passenger seat. I started the car, put it in reverse, backed it out, and drove down to the other side of the parking lot. Then I turned it around and headed back to the original parking space. I was pretty proud of myself! Clark was amazed. Then as I was parking the car, I turned a little too much and *almost* missed hitting the car next to us. We got out to survey the damage: a small dent in the right rear fender.

That evening at the dinner table, Dad stopped eating and said to me, "I understand you had a little problem today." I nodded my head while looking down at my plate. He continued, "Well, you'll need to pay to have their car repaired." I nodded my head again, still looking down. Again he spoke. "I will ask Skip to get somebody who can fix it—it shouldn't cost too much." Skip got it fixed, I paid a modest amount, and my parents never said another thing about it. More astonishing to me is that I never heard one word of chastisement—even in a joking way—from any of the Hinckley family. My hunch is that they discussed it at their dinner table that evening and decided as a family not to give me a hard time about my mistake.

Friends help us learn to forgive ourselves when we have made a mistake. They help us see beyond the trouble we are experiencing in the moment and gather strength to move forward. In many ways they build our faith just as parents build faith. They see us in our worst times and in our best. Whether they are friends during childhood and youth, as I was with Clark, or our adult friends, as my dad was with Skip, they help us navigate the sometimes difficult paths of life.

Research has shown that friendship attachments are influenced by the quality of a child's attachment to parents, but also by the quality of a mother's interpersonal relationships. In other words, children who feel safe and secure and have an enduring attachment with their parents find it easier to make friends as they grow to adulthood.[4] Parental love, as well as parental modeling, make it easier for children to make friends. Parents with avoidant or anxious attachment styles make it more difficult for their children to make friends with others and to form lasting family relationships. Friends are not simply a pleasant side effect of mortality; they are essential to one's happiness.

We sometimes think of friendship attachments lasting only through mortality, but I'm convinced that when true friendship happens, the attachment does not end at death. I believe that Skip and Wes have seen each other in the next life. Their friendship was like that of Zoram and Nephi's. As Lehi declared to Zoram, "I know that thou art a true friend unto my son, Nephi, forever" (2 Nephi 1:30). I take that word *forever* literally. When close attachments happen—whether they are made as children as mine was with Clark, as co-workers or mentor-mentee, or as missionary and convert—friends, like family members, can be with us eternally.[5]

4. Dorothy Markiewicz, Anna Beth Doyle, and Mara Brennden. "The Quality of Adolescents' Friendships: Associations with Mother's interpersonal Relationships, Attachments to Parents and Friends, and Prosocial Behavior," Journal of Adolescence 24: 429–445.
5. Henry B. Eyring, "Family and Friends Forever," *Ensign*, December 2013.

Because *eternal* means without beginning or end, we know that many of the lasting friendships we forge in this life had their beginning before we were born. As Elder Neal A. Maxwell has taught: "One of the reasons we love each other in the kingdom is that our friendships are not friendships of initiation at all but are, instead, friendships of resumption!"[6]

Thus the close, gospel-centered friendship attachments we make in mortality had their origin when we were in the pre-earth life jointly deciding to follow the plan of happiness given to us by a loving Father in Heaven and a willing Son. That happiness, as Elder Maxwell taught, included sacred, priceless friendships that we enjoyed long before we came to earth and that we will continue to enjoy forever.

Invitations:

See through your friend's eyes.
Look past outward differences to find another's inner beauty.
Never look down on another, always look up.
Accept what a friend cannot change.
Rekindle a friend's inner spirit.

6. Neal A. Maxwell, "Brim with Joy," BYU Speeches, . January 23, 1996, https://speeches.byu.edu/talks/neal-a-maxwell/brim-joy/

STAY SPIRITUALLY CLOSE

We are born in relationships,
wounded in relationships,
and heal in relationships.[1]

—Harville Hendrix

During the COVID-19 pandemic, we were admonished to socially distance ourselves from one another, making it more difficult to nurture and maintain relationships. But even though physical separation caused a certain amount of pain, many found ways to stay spiritually close. Separation anxiety is real. That is why spiritual closeness is so essential to our well being. An African woman, whom I will call Malu, came to the United States as a refugee and was separated from her parents at the age of thirteen. The following is my rendition of Malu's story told in her own voice:

> It was a long day, one I thought would never end. Mama was worried all day. She seemed to know that something bad was coming, but I didn't know what it was. I wondered if she was worried because our food was running out or because Papa had

---

1. Jason N Linder, "The Psycho-Physiology of Relationships: What You Don't Know," *Psychology Today*, July 12, 2020, https://www.psychologytoday.com/us/blog/relationship-and-trauma-insights/202007/the-psycho-physiology-relationships-what-you-dont-know

not returned since morning or because I was too lazy to help her when I woke up. I couldn't tell, but I knew it was something serious. As the sun began to hide behind the tallest trees, the heaviness of the air began to weigh down on me. Then I heard the "pop-pop-pop" of guns in the distance. I was only thirteen years old, but I knew the sound of enemy fire. I grew up knowing that the Hutus hated us because we were Tutsis, not because we had hurt them in any way, but just because we were Tutsis. You can see hate in people's eyes, just as you can see love. For generations the Hutus hated our tribe because we had ruled over them. Tutsis were the Jews of Africa, the ones the Hutus wanted to exterminate.

As the sound of war crept closer to our tent, Mama held me tighter and tighter. "It will be all right," she whispered. "I'm here, and I won't let you go." My head was cradled in the fatty part of her arm, making me forget for a moment the pending chaos that was approaching. Mama stood up, pushed me behind her dress as if to hide me from the enemy, but it was too late. The attackers were getting too close. "Malu," Mama yelled, "run, run to your uncle—he will protect you!" I saw my uncle only a few yards away. I ran and clung to his leg. He grabbed my hand and began to run. Then he picked me up and ran faster. "Mama! Mama!" I yelled. But when I turned to look back, she was falling to the ground, seemingly in slow motion. I began to scream and cry, but my uncle put his hand over my mouth. "We've got to keep moving. Stay quiet," he intoned. When we finally escaped the attack, I sat down in someone's tent I did not know and began to cry. I kept seeing my Mama falling to the ground over and over again. I knew she was dead, and I was sure that my father had also been killed, and nothing my uncle could do would bring them back. The tears would not stop. I cried all night.

I didn't understand until much later that my uncle had taken me across the border to Rwanda, a small country still reeling from civil war, a country where my tribe was no more welcome than we had been in the D.R. Congo. My aunt and most of my cousins were killed the night we fled to Rwanda. All I had now was my uncle. We kept moving from place to place without being able to find safety. The Tutsis were always on the run. Crossing another border to Burundi, we still hoped for a little peace, and for a few months I felt more calm. But the Hutus never disappeared. One day my uncle announced, "Malu, Kenya is our only hope. I've heard they have camps for us. We will begin our journey tomorrow."

The camps were crowded with other refugees from surrounding countries. I turned sixteen in Kenya, getting used to speaking Swahili, but we were living with others from my home country, so I kept my native tongue alive, and although my uncle and others had been constantly kind to me, my heart kept longing for Mama. Years after I saw her fall to the ground in a hail of gunfire, I ached for her to wrap me up in her arms and hold me until all the pain of our separation might drain out of me one tear at a time until all my tears were gone.

The refugee camp was hot and cramped, but somehow we found a way to endure it because it was our only option. Years came and went, and I kept longing for Mama even though I knew I would never see her again. At times I could hear her voice reassuring me that everything would be all right. Without that reassurance I don't think I would have applied for asylum. But I did, and it was granted. Fourteen years in Kenya, and all of a sudden I was on my way to the U.S. Shortly after my arrival in New York I heard my cell phone ring. Someone asked if I was Malu from Africa, and I confirmed that I was. Next I heard a voice, and my heart stopped, "Malu, it's Mama." I could not speak. Was someone imitating her? I didn't know what to think. Finally I got a few words to come out of my mouth. "Is that really you, Mama?" I questioned. "I thought you were dead, Mama." "I know," she replied. "I've been trying to find you ever since I was shot on that horrible night, but I couldn't find you. When I talked to the people in immigration, they asked if I had a daughter, and that's how I found you."

Tears came back, but there was no sadness in me. These were tears of astonishing relief, of unexpected rebirth, of sheer joy. My Mama was alive! And even though we couldn't touch each other physically, I felt close to her again. She was still in Africa and would remain there for several more years, but one day I would find a way to bring her to America where we could smile and laugh and eat together as we did when I was a young child.

My refugee friend was thirteen when she was separated from her mother, but what if separation occurs much earlier in a child's life? The following account comes from the experience of one of the thousands of mothers and children who were separated while trying to enter the U.S. illegally: "One woman, Miriam, from Guatemala, said she didn't have a chance to say a word to her 4-year-old son before he was taken from her at dawn while he was fast asleep—he was still asleep when they put him on a truck and drove away, she said. When she was finally able to reach him by phone, she said he refused to speak to her. The journalist was unable to confirm how much time had passed since their separation. But as Miriam tells it, it was long enough to make an impression on him. 'He's mad at me,' she said, tears in her eyes. 'He thinks that I abandoned him.'"[2]

The son's conclusion that his mother had abandoned him is understandable. He assumed that his mother had left him permanently. And he likely felt that his mother had left him because she no longer loved him. He felt rejected by the one he trusted most, the one he loved the most deeply. The boy's separation was starkly different from that of Malu's. Malu knew her mother loved her, even though she thought her mother had been killed. Her mother's last words to Malu were words of love, words of protection. But the Guatemalan boy had no final words from his mother before they were separated. He was taken away while asleep. At his young age, when he awoke in a strange place surrounded by people he had never seen before who spoke a different language, all he could conclude was that his own mother—the one he knew in his heart loved him—had deserted him because she did not want to be with him any longer.

Scenes of children being ripped away from their mothers—like the Guatemalan boy was—touched off a firestorm in the

---

2. Tal Kopan, "6 Children in 6 Days, Thousands Left: Inside the Family Reunifications," *CNN Politics,* June 27, 2018, https://www.cnn.com/2018/06/27/politics/six-children-families-separated-reunifications/index.html.

U.S. There is something unspeakably sacred about the relationship between a mother and a young child. Because the child is totally dependent on the mother, the forced separation causes tangible pain in anyone who witnesses it. Perhaps those who view the scenes are reflecting on their own childhood experiences with their mothers, or if they are now mothers they may be considering how violated they would feel if their child was forcefully taken from them. Whatever its causes, the outrage was real—all because of the bond, the relationship, the attachment between mother and child that should not be broken by anyone, least of all a nameless governmental agent.

When the Guatemalan boy and his mother were reunited, I assume that the wound of separation was gradually healed and that the son recovered his trust for his mother. But what if a mother leaves a child not because she is forced to but because she no longer wanted to care for the child? What if a child's feelings of being rejected and being unloved are based on fact, not fear? Or what if a mother continues to raise a child but has difficulty actually loving the child? What if the mother would leave if she felt she could?

My African friend never felt that her mother had abandoned her. Even though they could not be together, she knew deep down that if her mother had not been shot, they would still be together. She felt her mother's love even though she thought her mother was dead. But when children feel unloved, ignored, or abandoned by the mother, the consequences on the child's development can be incalculable.

Most would readily agree that a mother's or father's rejection or neglect of a child would seriously impact the child's emotional health. According to those who study attachment styles, a child who cannot trust a parent will also have difficulty trusting others, and a young child who suffers attachment problems will likely have attachment problems in adulthood. Simply stated, these professionals agree that our early years affect the way we relate to others as we grow older—that some develop a healthy, stable relationship style, while others develop an anxious or avoidant style.[3]

If his mother had never returned, the young boy who was separated from his mother at the border crossing might have developed an avoidant style, causing him to avoid close relationships and making it difficult for him to trust others. Many who have been deserted by those they most trust are often reluctant to trust others, and so they have difficulty forming relationships with anyone.

If Amanda, who spent her childhood in an orphanage, is like most children who are adopted, she will one day want to know more about her birth parents. She will likely want to know something of their physical characteristics and their likes and dislikes, and she will want to know why they gave her up for adoption. That parent-child attachment—even when it never forms between a child and birth parents—continues to affect the child. We want to know who we are, not only genetically, but personally, and somewhere down deep we know that a central feature of our own identity emerges from the attachments we have with those who gave us life—on earth and more significantly in heaven.

Invitations:

Stay spiritually close even when physically separated.
Nurture parental love.
Pray always for closeness to heavenly parents.

---

3. Jude Cassidy and Phillip R. Shaver, *Handbook of Attachment: Theory, Research, and Clinical Applications.* Third Edition (New York: The Guilford Press, 2016).

HOLD ON TO FAMILY

*When love extends from one generation to another,
all attachments are strengthened—
both human and divine.*

Parent-child and marriage relationships are crucial to our well-being in mortality and beyond, but all family attachments are important. Consider one's relationship with siblings. These brother and sister attachments can last longer than any other familial relationship. On average our parents will die twenty-five years before we do, but our siblings will be on earth after our parents have left us. Given the potentially long time siblings inhabit this world together, we may spend surprisingly little time thinking about the impact of these relationships on our own life.

Siblings can be among our closest relationships in mortality, but they can also be our most frustrating, painful relationships. A friend recently recounted how he was assigned to mediate a dispute between siblings over inherited property. The majority of the family members agreed on how the property should be divided, but two brothers felt shortchanged. As my friend moved between the two feuding groups, trying to resolve the dispute, he said, "I could soon see that they would never come to agreement; there was just too much negative history between the two sides." *Negative history.* A long pattern of dysfunctional relationships had caused a rift that could not or would not be healed. In the

Russell T. Osguthorpe

words of those who have studied the effects of our own history on relationships, "If we truly want to understand ourselves, we need to understand our history—our true history. Because the emotional residue of our past follows us."[1] And that residue affects our attachments either for good or ill.

We choose our friends, but we do not choose our siblings. Friends typically have much more in common with each other than do siblings, even though siblings may be more genetically similar than two friends. Even identical twins, raised in the same home at the same time, often become quite different as adults. However, unlike the siblings who battled over inherited property, sibling rivalry in childhood does not necessarily lead to dysfunctional relationships as adults. In fact, siblings who may not have related well as children because of age difference, for example, become best friends as adults. Negative history can be replaced by positive history. Rivalry can be turned into mutual support and love.

China's one-child policy, which was in force in some form from 1979–2016, basically precluded a significant portion of the population from the privilege of enjoying sibling relationships. If the parents could have only one child, there could be no brothers and sisters and eventually no cousins. Although demographers have discussed several negative results of the one-child policy, few if any have focused on the loss of siblings and hence the elimination of brother and sister relationships.[2] Rather, emphasis is usually placed on the parent-child relationship rather than on the relationships we experience as brothers and sisters.

In addition to sibling relationships, we form attachments with extended family members, such as aunts, uncles, cousins, and

1. Bruce D. Perry and Oprah Winfrey, *What Happened to You?: Conversations on Trauma, Resilience and Healing* (New York: Flatiron Books, 2021).
2. Lily Kuo and Xueying Wang, "Can China recover from its disastrous one-child policy?" *The Guardian*, 2019, https://www.theguardian.com/world/2019/mar/02/china-population-control-two-child-policy.

110

grandparents. I grew up next door to my Grandma Bessie, the only grandparent who lived long enough to develop a meaningful attachment to me. She taught me more about family relationships than I could otherwise have hoped to learn.

Grandma Bessie lived a long life and had time to influence me through all her days. A soft-spoken woman with indomitable inner strength, her example always seemed present in my mind. Life had not been easy for her, but those who knew her—even in fleeting encounters—felt only her strength and never her struggles. Always pleasant. Always thoughtful. She simply lived life as it came, even when it came with hard blows. As a young woman, she married Osmond, and they had four children. But when she was pregnant with her fifth child, Osmond became very ill. A serious infection? Cancer? No one was quite sure. He was surely seriously ill. Those close to him exercised their faith, especially Bessie.

Osmond was only thirty-four years old. Before the illness, he had been physically active and strong. So, Bessie fell to her knees, hoping, of course, that with her faith a miracle might occur. Bessie loved God. She knew that God knew of her love. She also knew that God knew how much she loved Osmond.

But the miracle did not come—no last minute recovery, no return of strength. At his side Bessie hoped one final time for a reprieve. But Osmond died in her arms. Osmond's passing was sad for everyone who knew him, although it was most difficult for the one who knew him best, Bessie. However, Bessie's story was not ultimately a sad one, because it didn't end with Osmond's death. Bessie kept going. Actually, she did much more than keep going. She never became bitter. She never lost her faith. She never expressed resentment about being widowed at the age of thirty-one while pregnant with her fifth child. Some might conclude that she had good reason to question God. She may have wondered why God seemed to have forgotten her, why He had not stepped in and saved Osmond. But she asked none of these questions. She simply went on to raise all five children, all of whom remained faithful throughout their lives.

When Osmond died, Bessie needed a home in which to raise her five young children. The lot next to her parents' home was large enough that a small house could be built for Bessie and her children. However, Osmond had no life insurance, so she had no funds to build the home. She continued to live with her parents, waiting for some sort of miracle, and this time the miracle came. The priesthood quorums of her ward volunteered their time to build the newly widowed mother a home so she could raise her family. She sustained herself by ironing laundry for the neighbors. Memories say that she got only five cents for each shirt she ironed, but by doing this she could earn enough for food and could care for her children.

The following are a few lines I wrote about my grandma Bessie.

Bessie

White shirts wrinkled and wadded,
Stacked in baskets, waiting to be pressed.
Her living room a laundry for the neighborhood.

Widowed at such an early age.
Left alone with four children
and one waiting to be born.

How did she do it?
Did she ever stop missing Osmond?
Did she ever complain?
Did she ever cry?

So soft on the outside, so strong on the inside.
So kind, so thoughtful, so giving.
Never expecting anything in return.

Alone for sixty-three years.
But she never seemed alone.
Never.
Accepting of everyone and everything.

She did not speak of Osmond,
So I asked her one day, "What was he like?"
"He was a good man."

I wanted more.
But maybe that's all anyone needs to be—
Good, just good.

Bessie was the only grandparent I remember. My mom's mother died when I was only one-and-a-half years old, so I have no memory of her. But surprisingly I remember Bessie's father, my great-grandfather. He died when I was three-and-a-half years old. He lived in a home adjacent to ours, and I remember walking with him up the dirt road behind our home on the way to the chicken coop. He would often sit on the back porch and talk to us as we were playing, warning us not to go into the shanty because we might get hurt. Of course, the more he tried to keep us out of that worn out little shed, the more we wanted to enter it. Tools galore were inside, old rusty tools that hadn't been touched for years.

Those who study attachment theory have shown that grandparents can influence a grandchild's parenting patterns through "intergenerational transmission."[3] A grandchild can see patterns of attachment in parents that are similar to those in the

---

3. Pietro De Carli, Angela Tagini, Diego Sarracino, Alessandra Santona, Valentina Bonalda, Paolo Elena Cesari, and Larua Parolin, "Like grandparents, like parents: Empirical evidence and psycholanlytic thinking on the transmission of parenting styles," *Bulletin of the Menninger Clinic 82*: https://guilfordjournals.com/doi/abs/10.1521/bumc_2017_81_11

grandparent, just as I could see those patterns in my father, my grandmother, and my great-grandfather. I remember watching as my great-grandfather spent his final days in bed. I can still see him lying there, his energy depleted, no longer able to sit on the porch and give us direction. The residue that remains from such memories still gives me strength. What is my most dominant memory of my great-grandfather? Kindness—the same kindness I felt from his daughter, my grandmother Bessie. He was kind to me as a three-year-old. I have a picture of him holding me in his arms. When I look at that picture I can feel his warmth, his acceptance, and yes, his love. I knew him for such a short time, but he influenced me in undeniable ways.

What about grandparents who died long before we were born? We all have them. We see them on our family tree. Can we form attachments with those we have never met? I am convinced that we can. The more we learn about their lives, the deeper the attachment becomes. One such ancestor for me is Lester Russell. He joined the Church in Nauvoo, married there, and had three children. His wife died not long after his last child was born. Valoran was the only one of Lester's children who survived. Then Lester remarried and began his trek across the plains with the other Saints on their way to a new life in the West. But shortly into the expedition, Lester died of cholera, leaving his young son Valoran to be raised by his grandfather, Daniel Russell. Had Valoran not survived and Daniel had not been willing to raise him, I would not have been born.

Do I feel an attachment to these ancestors I have never met? I cannot fully explain it, but yes, I do. When I read even the brief accounts that we have of their lives, I can feel their commitment, devotion, and strength. Do I believe that they have love for me even though we never met in mortality? Again, yes, I do. This love that transcends the veil between this life and the next is real. That is why prophets keep imploring us to seek out our ancestors. We do family history not only so we can perform ordinances for those who had no opportunity to receive them in this life but also so we can be strengthened by their love. Those who study epigentics (how features outside our genetic inheritance affect us) have concluded that "it is conceivable that the experiences of our grandparents, great-grandparents, and ancestors even further back have had a significant influence on the way we're going to express our DNA."[4] Secure, lasting attachments can form between two people who are living, two who are deceased, or between one who is living and one who has passed on. Attachments have no boundaries.

Invitations:

> *Deepen a relationship with a sibling.*
> *Connect more often with extended family members.*
> *Form attachments with grandparents on both sides of the veil.*

---

4.   Bruce D. Perry & Oprah Winfrey. 2021. *What Happened to You?: Conversations on Trauma, Resilience, and Healing.* New York: Flatiron Books.

BUILD UP THE SOUL

*It is easier to build strong children
than to repair broken [adults].*[1]

—Frederick Douglass

Mentoring relationships are often compared with parent-child relationships. Those with healthy, secure attachment styles form effective mentoring relationships much more easily than do those with insecure attachment styles. Stories of mentoring relationships that dissolve out of frustration between the mentor and the one being mentored are common and can often be traced to the insecure attachment style in either the mentor or the mentee. Contrarily, when the mentoring relationship is strong and secure, both mentor and mentee learn and grow together.

I have been blessed with a number of inspiring mentors during my life, and the attachments that have formed between us have influenced me positively in innumerable ways. Ideal mentors participate in what might be called a hybrid relationship: friend, parent, teacher, and guide in one strong, unselfish individual. One such mentor for me was Grant Von Harrison, who was my graduate program adviser. He was a builder in every sense of

---

1. Frederick Douglass, *Young Children*, Volume 53 (1964), 375, https://authenticamericandream.blogspot.com/2018/05/quote-investigation-frederick-douglass.html.

the word, making those he mentored believe that they could do more than they thought they could. And he mentored in so many different ways. When he noticed that one of the young men in his ward was struggling with the decision to serve a mission, he asked if he could be assigned to be his home teacher companion. To help the young man, Grant developed a set of introductory missionary lessons and helped him give them to multiple members of the ward. When the young man stood in sacrament meeting before departing for his mission, he said, "Without Brother Harrison, I would not be here today—I don't think I would have ever decided to go on a mission."

Grant was ministering before ministering was formally introduced by the Church. In fact, I believe he saw ministering and mentoring as nearly synonymous. One of my favorite examples of his "mentoring ministering" occurred shortly after he and his wife, Pat, retired and moved to St. George, Utah. Not long after they had become settled in their new home, Grant was called to home teach a less active family who lived nearby and had also recently moved to St. George. The family had several children, the oldest ones being teens. On his first visit to their home, Grant rang the doorbell and waited. Finally, the father in the home opened the door. "Hello, I'm your new home teacher," said Grant. The man looked at the floor, trying to get the words right: "We really don't need home teachers." Then Grant, in his typical forthright manner, responded, "Maybe you don't understand. I have been assigned to be your home teacher, so I need to see you and your family." Undaunted, the man responded, "Maybe you don't understand, we don't need home teachers." Finally, Grant, not wanting to get into an argument with his neighbor, handed him a piece of paper with his phone number and said, "Just call me when you're ready, and I'll be here."

Grant returned to his home and recounted the experience to Pat. A short time later, the phone rang. Pat answered and said, "Yes, he'll do that." She then told Grant that the neighbor had called and invited him to come back as soon as possible. Grant obliged. When his neighbor invited Grant in, Grant could see he was troubled. After listening to his story, Grant said, "So you are now able to live off the inheritance you received from your parents, so you haven't been working, right?" The man nodded. Grant then said, "You need work. You're depressed because you're not doing anything. You're young and you need work. I'll help you find something."

Grant further helped him with questions that had been troubling him about the Church and its teachings. After resolving these questions, Grant urged the man to return to activity, to become fully engaged in the Church again, and to bring his family with him. The man found an entry-level job and was soon promoted to a managerial position. He did return to Church, along with his wife and children. He and his wife were subsequently called to positions in the ward.

The family always revered Grant for the part he had played in helping them return to full activity in the Church. A few years passed, and one day while sitting toward the back of the chapel during sacrament meeting, Grant leaned on Pat and uttered something that Pat could not understand. Pat knew something was terribly wrong. The bishop was at the pulpit speaking and saw Pat wave her arm as if to call for help. Toward the front of the chapel the man Grant had home taught noticed the bishop's distress, turned and saw Pat, and quickly moved to the aisle and hurried to where Pat was struggling to hold Grant. He picked Grant up in his arms and carried him to the foyer. The bishop stopped the sacrament meeting, went to the foyer, and gave Grant a blessing while someone called an ambulance.

That was Grant's first stroke. He later had at least seven more. Each stroke stole a little more from him until finally he was bed-ridden, unable to walk, talk, or feed himself. A man who had been afraid of nothing was now in a tragic physical prison that permitted him to understand what others said to him but did not allow him to respond.

The image of the once-less-active man rushing to help save the one who had helped save him exemplifies for me what it means to be filled with God's love for our friends. Grant likely had little in common with the man he home taught. But they forged a friendship that endured.

While I was serving as Sunday School general president, some asked, "What is it like working with the General Authorities?" I was never quite sure what they expected to hear. I could have responded, "Well, it's work, real work, demanding work, and lots of it!" But I always felt that below the surface meaning of their question lay another question: "What are prophets, seers, and revelators really like when you are up close to them?" This was often my response: "Well, members of the Twelve and the First Presidency are each unique individuals. Their personalities are different from each other, but I've found one thing they have in common: They are all builders."

I would go on to explain that they were the most edifying people I had ever been around. Did they use candor? Were they frank in expressing their opinions? Yes. But did they use candor with kindness? Absolutely! And even more important, they gave honest praise to those around them; a staff member, a general officer (like me). It didn't matter—they were constantly building up the confidence of those around them.

Those who hold all the keys of the kingdom here on earth do not give random commendation or undeserved praise. They give abundant praise that is "deserved and specific."[2] It was Elder Neal A. Maxwell who specified these characteristics, and he did so on multiple occasions. Consider for a moment how this simple practice strengthens our relationship to God and to others. The parent who gives deserved specific praise to a child endears the child to the parent and brings them both closer to God. When others feel inadequate, which we all feel quite regularly, specific

---

2. Neal A. Maxwell, February, "Jesus, the Perfect Mentor," *Ensign*, February 2000.

praise that is well deserved can give them the impetus they need to carry on.

I recently heard about a musician who began his career with a mentor who believed in him more than he believed in himself. During the performer's first round of concerts, only a few people came to listen. His average attendance was ten. He was ready to give up, but his mentor kept encouraging him. During later rounds of performances, his average attendance grew to twenty. He approached his mentor and exclaimed, "See, no one wants to hear me!" His mentor's response? "Hey, let's be objective; your attendance has doubled!" So he continued. Eventually, he was playing to sell-out crowds every concert.

The mentor's praise was deserved and specific. He even cited the numbers that the musician saw as discouraging to show that he was actually making progress. My own mentor, Grant, did the same thing constantly, and so do those we sustain as prophets, seers, and revelators. Everyone needs more such praise, and everyone needs to give it more often. It builds the one receiving it and the one giving it. It is the stuff of strong, healthy, enduring attachments.

Invitations:

Recognize others' gifts.
Give more praise.
Mentor more.
Minister by lifting and building.

LET LOVE BE
THE MOTIVE

*To love as Christ loved is to love the Father
best of all, to obey Him to the end and
therein find the divine motivation to love
our neighbor as ourselves.
This was indeed a new idea.*[1]

—Jeffrey R. Holland

The story of the brother of Jared and his ministry is a story of love—love the Lord had for the Jaredites and the brother of Jared specifically, love that the brother of Jared had for the Lord, and love that the people had for each other, for their leader, and for the Lord, who was protecting and instructing them. Love was the power behind all of the actions that led them to journey to a new land, a land of promise. But when they arrived in Moriancumer, they momentarily stopped calling upon the Lord for direction, and their attachment to Him weakened.

---

1. "Elder Holland at Mission Leadership Seminar: The Savior summarized His ministry in 1 principle—'love one another'," *Church News,* June 27, 2020, https://www.thechurchnews.com/leaders-and-ministry/2020-06-27/elder-holland-mission-leadership-seminar-two-great-commandments-jo-seph-smith-martyrdom-187809.

The record is scant but revealing. For four years the Jaredites lingered on the seashore in their tents and seemed to forget about the purpose of their journey. They somehow lost their way because they lost their attachment to God, and their leader was slipping away as well. Then the Lord appeared in a cloud and spoke with the brother of Jared for a full three hours, giving him correction, getting him back on the right path, helping to reignite the relationship that had waned. As He always does, the Lord made it clear that He would forgive the brother of Jared and his people of their forgetfulness (their sins, at least of omission) if they would repent and call upon Him again.

The scene is instructive in so many ways. The Lord was helping this prophet of prophets understand that even though his love for the Lord was diminished during those four years, the Lord's love for him and for his people had never weakened one whit. The Jaredites had temporarily forgotten Him, but He had never forgotten them. Why did the Lord give correction to the brother of Jared and invite him to repent? Because God loves His children. Why had this prophet sought the Lord's direction to know how to help his people? Because the brother of Jared loved his people. Love was the motive behind every action that led the Jaredites to the promised land, just as love would later be the motive that would lead Lehi to leave Jerusalem and sail to the same new land (see Ether 1–5).

God the Father sent His Son to earth because He loved us, and the Savior carried out His mission on earth because He loved His Father and He loved us. This multi-directional and multi-dimensional love—the love that flows between the Father and the Son, the love that flows from them to us and back again, and the love that flows among all of God's children—is the motive for all to "fill the measure of their creation." This means that the quality of our loving relationships, our attachments, is the sum total of the quality of our life. When the Jaredites' attachment to God suffered, there is no doubt that their attachments with each other suffered. They drew away from God, and so it is inevitable that they became less loving toward others. The nearer we draw to God, the nearer we draw to others.

Every time we repent, we strengthen our attachment to God and to others. When we feel God's forgiveness, we want to forgive ourselves and others. When these feelings of forgiveness flow, attachments strengthen. One's ability to forgive and be forgiven is directly associated with attachment style. Those with avoidant style may have difficulty forgiving others. Those with an anxious style may have difficulty feeling forgiven. Once the brother of Jared had repented and felt God's forgiveness, his attachment to the Lord was strengthened. As his attachment to God strengthened, all he wanted to do was help his people repent, and then they immediately went to work on building more barges. Perhaps their inclination to collaborate on the work that they knew they needed to do had suffered in some way, because relationships are damaged when we distance ourselves from God.

When married couples neglect to nurture their relationship or choose not to care for their children, or when abuse occurs, we refer to them as "dysfunctional families." The Jaredites, during those four years became dysfunctional, forgetting their purpose in life and losing their desire to receive all of the blessings that the Lord had promised they would receive if they journeyed to a new, unknown land. Every person and every family have experienced these momentary lapses—times when they basically forget to express and receive love in ways that strengthen their attachment. The solution is to wake up, remember our purpose, and get to work to achieve it, just as the Jaredites did.

When Jesus lived on earth, He became our ultimate exemplar, experiencing the same mortal dilemmas, temptations, trials, and pain that every mortal faces. We marvel at the way He lived His life, the sermons He preached, the miracles He performed, and the mission He accomplished. But when those who worship Him as the Son of God focus on His outward acts, they might miss the most important message of His mortal life. His central message to all of us was not to amass a collection of actions or behaviors; His message was less concerned with what we do than with why we do it. He lived a perfect life on earth not because He preached the Sermon on the Mount or fed the five thousand or raised Lazarus from the dead—as inspiring as all of those events can be. His life was perfect because His motive was perfect, and that motive was love.

The Savior's motive needs to be our motive every day, all the time. When we were raising our family, one of our ward members was the chief executive officer of a billion-dollar corporation, yet he lived in a modest neighborhood, drove an inexpensive car, and dressed like all the rest of us. No one could tell by his outward behavior that he was an extremely wealthy man. As neighbors we sometimes wondered why he did not spend more of his money on himself. One day, while I was pumping gas into my car at a nearby cut-rate gas station, I looked up and saw our rich ward member pumping gas into his car. He recognized me and said, "I always come here—cheapest gas in town!"

I was serving in the Young Men organization at the time and asked him to speak at a fireside for youth. He accepted the invitation and began his talk by briefly explaining his personal history. As he was recounting his past, he mentioned the birth of a child with multiple disabilities into their family. When he invited the young people to pose questions, one of the young men asked, "How did you become so successful?" He paused for a moment before answering and then explained, "I've never thought of myself in those terms. When our child with disabilities was born, I knew that I would need to make enough money to help care for him, and so that was why I began my work as an entrepreneur. I knew he would need continued support even after I was gone."

The young man did not seem satisfied with the answer and then asked, "But was that the only reason you made so much money?" "No," he responded, "there was another reason—I found that I enjoyed providing jobs for other people so that they could raise their families. You see, I've never been interested in making money for myself. That never drove me. It was what I could do for others that kept me going."

This very wealthy man was saying that money was not his motive. If I had asked him to describe his motive, he likely would not have said, "Love." And that's the point—we seldom look at our own motives. We look at our actions, our to-do lists, our accomplishments, but we seldom sit back and ask, "Why am I doing this?" or "Why do I want to do that in the future?" If we do ask ourselves those questions, we may not look deeply enough to discover our actual motives. There are surface motives, and there are deeper motives. I might conclude that I'm earning a living so I can provide for my family, or I'm ministering to a sister or brother in the ward because they have certain needs. But these are only surface motives. Going deeper, we might ask ourselves if we're earning a living because we love our family and because we love others who are able to earn a living because of our efforts, as did the wealthy brother in my ward. Are we ministering to others because we love them, not simply because they have needs?

Are we getting down to the motive that the Savior taught us to live by? Speaking to newly called mission presidents and their wives, Elder Jeffrey R. Holland said, "The undeviating bond the Savior has with the Father is one of the sweetest things in the scriptures to have grown on me in recent years."[2] His declaration should cause us all to pause. Here is a member of the Twelve explaining that the relationship—the attachment or "undeviating bond," as he calls it—between the Father and the Son has been a scriptural image that he has savored in the scriptures during the past few years. This disciple has studied the scriptures as deeply as any modern follower of the Savior. He can express himself as clearly and powerfully about any gospel principle you

2. Ibid.

may request. And he has been focusing on the Father-Son attachment, Their "undeviating bond."

One reason the love between the Father and Son is so meaningful to all of us is that it shows the type of love—the kind of motive—we personally must aspire to in our own lives. Even though we know that we cannot attain to the ultimate love that They share, the goal still pulls us—partly because of the scriptural invitation to pray with all our hearts that we can be filled with the pure love of Christ (see Moroni 7:47–48). That invitation makes it clear that we can look inside our own heart to determine why we think what we think and do what we do, and determine if our actions are motivated by love.

Invitations:

Look inside.
Ask why you do what you do.
Let go of lesser reasons.
Then let love be the motive.

ELIMINATE VENGEANCE

*The problem that we have with a victim mentality
is that we forget to see the blessings of the day.
Because of this, our spirit is poisoned
instead of nourished.*[1]

—Steve Maraboli

The scene is familiar in most young families: Two children fighting. "He hit me!" "She hit me first, Mom!" "No, he was the one who started it!" Each child is sure that hitting back is fully justified, because their sibling landed the first blow. They have every right to hit back, not just to defend themselves from getting pummeled but because they have a right to retribution, or as the scriptures call it, vengeance. Likewise, spouses on the verge of divorce often blame their partner for the dissolution of their marriage. The more one blames the other, the greater the feeling of vengeance, and the greater the feeling of vengeance, the more the spouse feels a need to punish the other for destroying the marriage.

Vengeance is a fascinating phenomenon. The victim has the right to inflict injury on the one who inflicted injury first. It

---

1.   Steve Maraboli, *Unapologetically You: Reflections on Life and the Human Experience* (Port Washington, New York: A Better Today Publishing, 2013).

goes beyond childhood to the middle school bully, to the high school tough guy, and finally to domestic abuse and other criminal activities. It is a dangerous emotion leading to a wide variety of human pain. It has no positive outcome. Those who inflict injury on another never feel good; they may feel vindicated or relieved, but never good. This is why the Lord says, "Vengeance is mine"—not yours but mine. Eliminate it from your array of emotional reactions (see Mormon 8:20).

If the motive behind every good action is love, then the motive behind every vengeful action is hate or anger. So, in essence, the Lord is counseling that when we are injured by someone else we should avoid anger or lashing out of any kind. Such emotional reactions distance us not only from the one we are trying to injure but from God as well. Vengeance and all the punishing actions that accompany it can destroy relationships.

You may not know the name Victoria Ruvolo, but you may have heard her story. This woman was driving down a New York highway when an eighteen-year-old college student threw a frozen turkey at her car, smashing the windshield and severely injuring her. She was in a coma for two weeks and suffered long-lasting health conditions from the incident. But when the case came to the court, Victoria pled for leniency for the young man who threw the turkey. She did not want to "see him rot in jail."[2] As he pronounced the judgment, the presiding judge described how the capacity of Victoria Ruvolo to forgive the eighteen-year-old young man who had injured her had been impressive to others who had read about the case and had changed him personally.

We see many cases in the news daily about the vengeful reaction. So someone like Victoria Ruvolo captures our attention. Leaving the courtroom after the judgment had been pronounced, the young man approached Ruvolo, began weeping openly, put his arms around her, and repeated again and again,

---

2. Victoria Ruvolo , Robert Goldman, *No Room for Vengeance in Justice and Healing* (New York: No Vengeance Publishing, Inc., 2011).

"I'm so sorry! I am so sorry!" Those who witnessed this scene or heard about it must likely ask themselves if they would have reacted as this woman did. Would they have been as eager to forgive their assailant? Would they hold any rancor because of his thoughtless action? Would they want to see him hurt like they had been hurt?

Ruvolo clearly did not have an avoidant attachment style. Those with such patterns often blame others for their problems and in some cases want to see them punished for their actions. Ruvolo's actions showed that she had no problem empathizing with the one who had injured her. Her empathy overcame her hurt, literally erasing any feelings of vengeance. The more secure our attachment is, the easier we find it to empathize with another, and the more we free ourselves from any feelings of vengeance.

Most of us are unlikely to have our windshield hit by a frozen turkey, but at times we all feel hurt by the actions of someone else. At such moments we have two basic choices: forgiveness or vengeance. The first leads to an increase of love: initiation or strengthening of an attachment. The second leads us to what has been called a victim mentality. Most people are victims of negative events in their lives, but if we develop a victim mentality—always blaming outside faults or influences on our misfortune or pain—we run the risk of separating ourselves from God and from others.

Elder David A. Bednar has described how he has visited "hundreds and hundreds" of less active members of the Church to help them return to full activity. During these visits he found that the vast majority of those who had become less active described some situation or interaction that "offended" them. The way they dealt with the offense ("got back" at those who offended them) was to stop going to church. Taking offense can cause one to have vengeful feelings. Summarizing his message about offense, Elder Bednar reminded us that taking offense is a personal choice: "It ultimately is impossible for another person to offend you or to offend me. Indeed, believing that another person offended us is fundamentally false. To be offended is a choice we make; it is not a condition inflicted or imposed upon us by someone or something else."[3]

Elder Bednar's counsel is similar to that given earlier about making our own emotions. The person giving offense—even if that person meant to offend us—is not the one responsible for how we let ourselves feel. The Lord basically says, "Give those feelings of offense to me. Let me worry about any punishment that the person deserves. Your job is to forgive not punish. Remember, vengeance is mine."

When my grandmother's husband died at the age of thirty-four, she could have reacted very differently than she did. She could have felt forgotten by God, even offended by him. She could have blamed God for her misfortune because there was no one else to blame. She could have developed a victim mentality. But rather than letting the event paralyze her, she somehow miraculously let it strengthen her. She allowed the Lord to heal her pain, renew her confidence, and give her determination to carry on and raise her family as a single mother. Her inner strength helped others be stronger, just as Victoria Ruvolo's strength in forgiving helped so many, including the judge, look inside and find a reservoir of forgiveness that they had not previously recognized. The more we can find that inner strength—a strength that comes from our attachment to God, from allowing the power of His Atonement to change us—the less we will be offended and the more we will strengthen others and their relationships with one another.

Invitations:

> *Let the Lord heal you.*
> *Let go of the pain of the past.*
> *No revenge, no getting back,*
> *Only forgive.*

---

3. David A. Bednar, "And Nothing Shall Offend Them," *Ensign*, November 2006, https://www.churchofjesuschrist.org/study/general-conference/2006/10/and-nothing-shall-offend-them?lang=eng.

REMEMBER LOVE

The more you remember Him,
the more you will feel His love.
And the more you feel His love,
the more you will want to
share that love with others.

There are moments in everyone's life when love holds sway, when no outside force, however strong it might be, can steal our love for God or our compassion for another. In contrast, most have the opposite kinds of moments when frustration or anger overcomes love and we act in ways we would like to forget. Remembering the positive moments can often build a pathway to increasing our capacity to love. Healthy, stable, secure attachments have many of those positive moments, and the more we dwell on those, the more we can strengthen our present relationships with God and with others. Remembering times when we have felt His love will help us feel it more now. Remembering times when we felt love from our spouse, child, sibling, or friend can strengthen that relationship now. Attachments are not stagnant or one-dimensional; they are multi-faceted and always changing—either becoming stronger or weaker. So, building on our past by focusing on those positive moments can lead to unforeseen joys in the present.

When Moses led the children of Israel out of Egypt, he did it out of love for God and for his people. Moses felt God's love, and so he had to act on it. God's love was the underlying power that delivered the Israelites from bondage and from total captivity. But as soon as the Israelites had been delivered, they began to forget the very power that had delivered them. They forgot that seminal, miraculous moment of God's love for them. Forgetting His love literally broke their attachment to God, and they began worshipping idols: lifeless, loveless golden statues that they could see with their eyes and touch with their hands. The more they forgot God's love for them, the harder their own hearts became. Not only did they lose their attachment to God, but they also lost their attachments to his prophet and to their fellow Israelites.

Outward influences, such as hunger and thirst, wore the Israelites down, even when mana came from heaven and water came from a rock. They began focusing on negative forces rather than remembering the miraculous love from God that fueled their deliverance. They basically suffered from spiritual amnesia, as if their memory of the positive aspects of deliverance had been completely erased.

In a book entitled *The People's Republic of Amnesia,* the author showed young people the well-known picture of the Chinese man standing only a few feet away from an approaching tank and asking them if they recognized the photo.[1] The remarkable thing about the photo was that one Chinese man stopped a whole line of tanks in their tracks, because the driver of the lead tank could not run over one of his fellow citizens. Most American adults who were alive in 1989 would remember this photo, but the Chinese people did not recognize it. Newspapers in China were prohibited from publishing the photo because the image was associated with the slaughter of hundreds of student protestors that occurred the next day on Tiananmen Square.

I was not in Beijing when the tanks attacked the student protestors, but two weeks before the attack I was there conducting a workshop at Beijing Normal University. On the way to the university I watched thousands of students march along the street

---

1. Louisa Lim, *The People's Republic of Amnesia* (New York: Oxford University Press, 2014).

with pro-democracy placards. At the peak of one of the marches, the streets were packed curb-to-curb with students full of excitement and hope. A professor from Vanderbilt University, one of the workshop leaders, accompanied me to the highest floor of the Beijing Hotel so we could get a better view of what was happening on the square below us. We sat and watched for several hours. Students kept flowing like a river toward the square.

At one point soldiers began forming a line in front of the square, like a dam to stop the river of students. But the students kept flowing toward the square. Then, both my colleague and I had difficulty making sense of what we were seeing. Students kept moving and pleading with the soldiers to let them in. Without any struggle, the soldiers suddenly seemed to side with the students—no shots fired, no fighting. Then the line of soldiers broke, creating a large opening for students to pass freely, as if they were welcoming their friends into the square.

The soldiers' kindness was similar to the soldier in the news photo who stopped his tank before that courageous man. These were both signs of love of one Chinese citizen for another. Love held sway. Love continued to fuel the energy of students in our seminar as they took water to their peers so they would not die from fasting. I am certain that those who participated in that historic protest never forgot the kindness shown to them by the soldiers who let them enter the square or to their friends who literally kept them alive while they fasted for a change in their government.

All relationships have positive and negative moments. The ongoing quality of the relationship depends on how we handle those events, not only when they are occurring but when we reflect on them weeks, months, and years later. Memory is essential to the strengthening of a relationship. If a husband and wife reflect on their relationship effectively, they can come to new levels of understanding, deepening their love for each other. If they permit outward forces or distractions to erase the memory of important moments in the relationship, their attachment may weaken. Some negative events require forgiveness and then forgetting, but some that seem negative when they occur can be stepping stones to improvement if remembered appropriately. And the positive moments? They should be celebrated regularly.

Those who study attachment have discovered that couples remember positive and negative events differently depending on their attachment style. In one study those with attachment avoidance focused more on the negative events in their marriage, remembering more details of those events than did those with an anxious attachment who more often focused more on the positive events. In addition, those who were highly avoidant, even though they remembered many details of the negative event, had trouble describing it in a coherent way. Their memory regarding the event was perhaps less accurate than it might have been.[2] Those with an avoidant style have difficulty trusting others, which might lead to their tendency to over-emphasize the negative events in their marriage, blaming their partner for difficulties rather than taking responsibility for the negative event themselves.

Those with healthy, stable attachments can remember positive and negative events in their relationship more accurately, more coherently, and more compassionately than those who are avoidant or anxious. More important, those who have developed an anxious or avoidant approach to their attachments can change, and that change will be more lasting and more fulfilling if they learn to reflect on their relationship—both the hard times and the good—with understanding and love.

During their occupation by the Egyptians, the Israelites needed to reflect more on God's love for them than on the evil acts of those who had hurt them. Likewise we need to focus our attention on acts of love we have experienced and not dwell on the negative moments in our relationships. The more we nurture this type of reflection, we will remember the love that God and others have shown, and we will strengthen our attachments.

---

2.   Wang Y, Wang Q, Wang D, and Feeney BC, "How Do I Narrate My Marriage: The Relationship Between Attachment Orientation and Quality of Autobiographical Memory," *Front Psychol.* 2018;9:2107. Published 2018 Nov 1. doi:10.3389/fpsyg.2018.02107

As discussed in an earlier chapter, covenants are the flesh and bone—the invisible fiber—forming our attachments to God and to others. Making the baptismal covenant is a one-time event, but the Lord provided the ordinance of the sacrament and proxy baptisms to help us remember that covenant any day of the week. The covenants we make in the temple then build on that original covenant we make when we become members of the Church. Remembering the commitments we make to each other when we are sealed in the temple keeps our marriage alive and growing. Reflecting on the words in that ordinance reminds us of the beauty of eternal attachments and helps us nurture the richness of our relationship throughout our marriage.

Returning to the temple often will help ensure that we do not suffer from temporary spiritual amnesia that can weaken our relationship with God and with others. Simply entering the temple and feeling God's love in that sacred place reminds us of our eternal nature and potential to love more as He loves, to forget our failures and remember our destiny as His sons and His daughters. Then, as we contemplate the covenants we have made in that sacred edifice, the impact of His love for us will continue to grow. The temple is an antidote to spiritual amnesia.

As President Russell M. Nelson has taught, "Every woman and every man who makes covenants with God and keeps those covenants, and who participates worthily in priesthood ordinances, has direct access to the power of God. Those who are endowed in the house of the Lord receive a gift of God's priesthood power by virtue of their covenant, along with a gift of knowledge to know how to draw upon that power."[3]

Invitations:

Remember the pain of captivity,
the joy of deliverance,
the freedom of God's mercy,
and the power of His grace.

---

3.   Russell M. Nelson, "Spiritual Treasures," *Ensign,* November 2019.

TREASURE
THE STORIES

Our stories give us grounding.
They transform our experience to roots.
They harvest fruits where there was once only mud.
They contain the seeds of what's to come.[1]

—Leah Pellegrini

A newly engaged couple is often asked, "How did you meet?" Family, friends, and even strangers want to know how the relationship between the two began, what brought them together, and how they decided to make their relationship permanent. These are attachment stories, perhaps the most important stories of one's life. The couple may recount their story often prior to their marriage, and they will continue to recount it throughout their married life. Attachment stories—either to a spouse, to a child, to a friend, or to God—are the stories that bring the most meaning into our lives, the stories that define us and help us fulfill our purpose on earth.

Everyone has attachment stories from their childhood. Some of these stories are happy, life-giving experiences. Jane Goodall,

---

1. Leah Pellegrini, "Our Stories Give Us Grounding," 2020, https://thecorestories.com

the naturalist who studied chimpanzees in Africa, recounted a happy childhood story recalled when she was four years old. She wanted to know where on a chicken was an opening big enough for an egg to come out. She was so determined to find an answer to her question that she crawled into a henhouse, hid in a pile of straw, and waited and watched for four hours until a chicken finally came in and laid an egg right in front of her.

Goodall described her mother's reaction when she returned home. "I was oblivious of the fact that no one had known where I was, and that the whole household had been searching for me. They had even called the police to report me missing. Yet despite her worry, when [my mother] still searching, saw [me] rushing toward the house, she did not scold me. She noticed my shining eyes and sat down to listen to the story of how a hen lays an egg: the wonder of that moment when the egg finally fell to the ground. . . . It is quite extraordinary how clearly I remember that whole sequence of events."[2]

I believe that Jane Goodall remembered that attachment story so well because it was the beginning of her curiosity about the animal world, a curiosity that eventually led her to become one of the best known naturalists of our time. Her mother could have reacted differently. She could have been angry at Jane for disrupting her day, for causing her to worry so much. But she didn't. She provided the secure base that is essential to healthy human development. Jane's mother actually encouraged her four-year-old to be inquisitive, which surely increased young Jane's confidence that she could learn about the world through observation and discovery.

Some attachment stories are less positive than Jane Goodall's. Some can be painful or even traumatic. The happy stories of childhood can lead to happiness in adult life, and the sad stories not dealt with can bring serious challenges in adulthood,

---

2.   Jane Goodall, *Reason for Hope* (New York: Warner Books, 1999), 6–7.

particularly affecting one's ability to form lasting, healthy attachments to others. Positive attachment stories, like Goodall's, need to be retold often. Negative attachment stories need to be recognized, but rather than dwelling on them, we need to be released from them and healed from them. At times experiences from our past are mystifying; we cannot quite discern why something happened the way it did, or why someone said or did something that disturbed us in some way. These experiences need to be unpacked, laid out, and clarified so that healing can come. Otherwise, we cannot move forward with faith and reassurance that our future will be better than our past.

The Restoration can be viewed through the lens of attachment stories. I have sometimes wondered what might have happened if young Joseph Smith's experience had been different following the First Vision. The first person to see Joseph following the vision was his mother, who had recently joined the Presbyterian Church. When she saw her son, she thought that something must be wrong, so she "inquired what the matter was." Then Joseph replied, "Never mind, all is well—I am well enough off. I have learned for myself that Presbyterianism is not true" (Joseph Smith—History 1:20). In his history Joseph did not go on to recount the rest of the conversation, but we know that his mother was accepting—even though her fourteen-year-old son was telling her that she had joined the wrong church. There is no indication that she became angry. Rather, she supported her son in his experience. Similarly, when Joseph described Moroni's visitation to his father, Joseph again was met with complete acceptance: "I returned to my father in the field, and rehearsed the whole matter to him. He replied to me that it was of God, and told me to go and do as commanded by the messenger" (Joseph Smith History—1:50).

The young prophet's parents were equally supportive of him, but others became hostile at the first mention of a heavenly visitation. Joseph faced opposition from the very beginning of his mission, but he had the sustaining influence of both parents, as well as from the Lord, to give him the strength and courage he needed to accomplish what he had been called to do.

Joseph's true and faithful relationships with the Lord, his parents, and other heavenly messengers made the restoration of the gospel of Jesus Christ possible. Had he not been able to form those bonds, he would not have been able to be the conduit through which truth could flow. The Book of Mormon itself is another evidence of attachment. Some outside the Church of Jesus Christ believe that Joseph wrote the book himself, but Joseph never wavered from his testimony that he was only the instrument of translation, which was performed by the gift and power of God. Without Joseph's impenetrable attachment to the Lord, he would not have been able to translate the characters on the plates.

There is always a positive power in attachment stories that reminds us of the love that God and others have for us. The stories can tie us to the past, and those ties can give us strength to move forward. We may come to see that we are writing new attachment stories every day. Our bonds with loved ones and our attachment to God can be either strengthened or weakened by our everyday thoughts and actions. Remembering stories of the past and writing stories of the present, we face whatever comes. All we need to know is that the Lord's love will lead us and lift us so we can write stories of acceptance, support, and encouragement—stories that will remind us of our eternal attachment to God and His children.

Invitations:

> *Treasure positive attachment stories.*
> *Recount them often.*
> *Let them bring bring joy.*
> *Keep writing new ones.*

RECOGNIZE
GOD'S HAND

Asking for and receiving daily bread
at God's hand plays a vital part
in learning to trust Him
and in enduring life's challenges.[1]

—D. Todd Christofferson

While speaking in a stake leadership training meeting, I invited a volunteer to join me at the podium. A young father came forward, and I asked him, "Is there anything you would like to do in your life that you have found difficult—something you really want to do but have not yet achieved?" He thought for a moment and said, "Yes, I want to spend more time with my family. My work has kind of captured me for the past few years. That's what I want to do—spend more time with my wife and kids." I responded, "Would it help if you reported back to me on how you're coming along with your goal?" He nodded in the affirmative. Then I concluded: "So you decide when you've made some progress, and let me know how it went." He agreed.

---

1.   D. Todd Christofferson, "Recognizing God's Hand in Our Daily Blessings," *Ensign*, January 2012.

Approximately one month later I received a two-page-small-print email message describing his progress. I read the message with particular interest because not only had this brother responded as he said he would, but the message showed that this simple invitation had led to a significant change in his life. "I want to let you know," he explained, "that because of that conversation we had in that training meeting I have experienced one of the greatest changes ever in my life. My marriage is stronger and happier, our kids are happier, and I'm happier." He went on to describe how he had day by day adjusted his schedule at work so he could spend more time with his family. Then he described how each morning when he awoke, he would thank God for the strength he had been given to change his life.

On another occasion I approached a single woman who had recently joined the Church. The missionaries who brought the gospel into her life had shared with me the challenges she had faced on the way to her baptism, including many personal lifestyle changes she had had to make. After she bore her testimony in a sacrament meeting, I approached her and said, "I'm so impressed with your strength and determination to do what you needed to do to become a member of this Church." She looked a bit surprised and responded, "Oh, don't feel sorry for me because of the changes I've made—giving up smoking and alcohol, giving up my boyfriend, cleaning up my language. Hey, these are nothing compared to what I have received by joining this Church! I used to wake up in the morning and go to work, come home, eat dinner, and go to bed. My life had no purpose at all. Now it has meaning! Now I know why I am alive!"

In both of these instances individuals were recognizing the hand of the Lord in their life. They acknowledged God's power, both His grace and His mercy—the power to act in new ways and the power to be forgiven of past mistakes. Those who recognize God's hand in their lives automatically, inevitably feel the Lord's love for them. The more they recognize His hand, the more they are filled with His love. It is more than a general gratitude. It is a specific awakening, a realization that God is mindful of them, that He knows their needs, as well as their gifts, and that He is eager to help them because He loves them.

Ammon's account in the Book of Mormon, when he begins to reflect on how much the Lord had blessed the sons of Mosiah and their companions in their missionary work, is as strong a demonstration of the importance of recognizing the hand of the Lord as can be found in all of scripture. "Don't you think we should celebrate? Think how the Lord has blessed us! Think of it—all of these converts are in God's hands, and He will one day raise them up. We should praise God! Because if we had not decided to serve our mission together, these new converts would still hate us."

Then Aaron says, "Hey, Ammon, don't you think you're getting a little carried away? Sounds like you're bragging!" But Ammon responds, "Aaron, you can't stop me. I'm just going to keep praising God for how He's helped us. We have felt the power of His word inside our hearts, so how can we keep from rejoicing? Do you remember how really bad we were? God snatched us away from our sinful state. God not only helped us bring thousands of Lamanites to a knowledge of the truth, but He totally forgave us of our sins. So how can we keep from singing His praises? How could we not be completely full of joy?" (See Alma 26.)

The image of being "snatched" does not usually come to mind when one thinks of the process of forgiveness. One typically thinks of the word *snatched* as meaning grabbed or plucked. But in this verse it clearly means rescued. I like the image of someone hanging onto the edge of a cliff, when the one above kneels down on top of the cliff, reaches over the edge, grasps the struggling hiker, and lifts her to safety.

The entire record of Ammon recounting his blessings is an inspiring message about the centrality of relationships. The sons of Mosiah turned against their faithful father and preached against the Church, but the Lord loved them enough to provide them with an angelic visitation that brought them to repentance. They were so transformed by the experience that they served a mission to the most hostile people they could possibly be called to teach. But they learned to love the Lamanites, and that love led to conversion. Then the new converts loved them back. Through it all, the sons of Mosiah, as well as their Lamanite converts, not only loved one another, but their love for the Lord grew exponentially.

Ammon and the sons of Mosiah literally changed their attachment style from one that was self-absorbed and avoidant to one that was submissive, loving, and enduring. They had distanced themselves from God because they felt no need for Him in their lives, and relied on others primarily for their own self-centered aims. Then, after their hearts had been changed by heavenly intervention, they turned their avoidant attitude into an enduring love for God and His children. Their example shows that anyone can change an avoidant or anxious style into a healthy, enduring attachment style by recognizing God's hand.

As Ammon recounted the Lord's blessings, His love for the Lord clearly increased, and so did His love for others. If we want to strengthen our attachment to God and to others, we need to recognize the hand of God in our lives every day. Upon awaking we can reflect for a moment on the blessings of yesterday, and we can look forward to the blessings that await us on the new day that is dawning. As we do, we will be filled with the Lord's love.

Invitations:

Reflect daily.
See the Lord's hand.
Give thanks for His boundless love.
Feel His love.

LIVE IN MERCY
AND GRACE

*We are to "seek this Jesus of whom the prophets
and apostles have written, that the grace of
God the Father and also the Lord Jesus Christ,
and the Holy Ghost which beareth record of them,
may be and abide in us forever."*[1]

—Julie B. Beck

I was once assigned to give a talk to the inmates in a high secu-rity prison. I can't say that I was particularly comfortable as I approached the sprawling facility with "pods" to keep the inmates as far away from each other as possible. Entering the building, I was greeted by a guard who had me empty all my pockets and deposit everything in a locker before going in. He then directed me through the metal detector, as I was greeted by another guard who explained that she would be escorting me to a small room where an inmate was waiting to interview me.

The interviewer was a man of perhaps thirty-something years, of medium build with light thinning hair and a nice smile. He

---

1.   Julie B. Beck and Danielle B. Wagner, "Sister Beck Shares How to Develop the Faith of Miracles, Become 'Awash in Christ's Grace'," *LDS Living*, May 2, 2019, https://www.ldsliving.com/Sister-Beck-Shares-How-to-De-velop-the-Faith-of-Miracles-Become-Awash-in-Christ-s-Grace/s/90751

stood politely to greet me when I entered the room and then explained that he would be introducing me in the meeting that was to follow. Asking lots of questions about my background and family, he seemed very engaged and situationally present. After he had finished I said, "I'm probably not supposed to ask this, but how long do you have left in here?" There was an awkward pause, and then he looked at the floor and responded in an almost inaudible tone, "Oh, I'm never getting out of here." His response actually surprised me. In the back of my mind, I must confess that I began wondering if I was talking to a serial killer.

We were sitting very close to each other. He raised his gaze from the floor and looked me in the eye. With tears streaming down his face, he said, "This is the best place for me. I can't control myself on the outside. That's why I need to be here for the rest of my life." Now I was doubly surprised. Not only did I not expect him to say he was in for a life sentence, but I did not expect him to show so much emotion. Weren't "hardened criminals" supposed to be hardened or "past feeling"? Looking back, I'm chagrined to think that my view of these inmates was so negatively influenced by media stereotypes.

My surprises continued as we entered the meeting room and saw upwards of fifty prisoners seated quietly. I learned that they had all come to the meeting completely voluntarily. No one was there who did not want to be there. The opening prayer was given, and then an inmate stood at the podium and read a beautiful, moving poem he had written about redemption, forgiveness, and the Lord's mercy. The inmate who had interviewed me then stood and introduced me to the group. He spoke with clarity and confidence. During these opening moments of the meeting I kept asking myself, "Are all of these people actually criminals?" Because they didn't seem like criminals.

Before I spoke, again to my surprise, a male chorus assembled at the front of the room and sang a hymn. The choir was exceptionally talented. Intonation was perfect, the director was highly skilled, and the performance was flawless. I learned later that this was an "audition only" choir. The director accepted only the most capable singers in the prison.

When I began speaking, I asked if anyone could recount the story of the sons of Mosiah preaching the gospel to the Lamanites. Hands went up all over the room. I called on several to give their renditions of the missionary account. For a moment I felt as if I was back in a zone conference as a mission president teaching my own missionaries. These prisoners were knowledgeable in the scriptures. Some cited multiple verses as they recounted how the sons of Mosiah found success among a hostile people.

The meeting ended, and I retrieved my personal items from the locker and drove away from the prison. As I was driving home I kept thinking of the words of one of my mentors, Arthur Henry King. In one of our conversations he became very intent and leaned forward on his chair: "I want you to remember something. I don't want you ever to forget it. Every person has good inside them. That includes every inmate in a prison."

At the time he said it, I wasn't sure what had motivated his comment. It seemed to come out of nowhere. But driving away from that prison, I began to understand. I had expected criminals to resemble the popular images that most of us have of murderers and rapists—hard-hearted, unrepentant, emotionless people. But that was not what I had found that day in that prison. It seemed that everyone I encountered had more than "some" good inside them—they had *a lot* of good inside them. Yes, they had made serious mistakes, but that did not mean they were beyond being helped, that they should be written off by the rest of society. No one is beyond the reach of the Savior's Atonement. This understanding, I believe, is what Brother King was trying to teach me.

My experience in that prison has so many implications for how we relate to each other. Healthy, lasting relationships are rooted at the deepest level in mercy. The inmates I encountered had made mistakes punishable by law, but all of us make mistakes that can weaken, injure, or even kill a relationship all together. The inmates had injured or killed others physically, but everyone can do things or say things that injure or kill others figuratively so that a relationship either suffers serious damage or dissolves completely.

At the end of the Book of Mormon, when Mormon could hardly bear the scene of carnage that confronted him every day—armies raping, killing, and even eating the flesh of the fallen—he said something that has always had great impact: "For I know that they [those killing each other] must perish except they repent and return unto him." This simple statement, which is repeated often in scripture, gives us all hope that no matter what mistake we make, we can be forgiven. It also reminds us to look at others—all others—in ways that amplify the good inside them rather than focusing on the bad. This also applies to the way we view ourselves. Being unable to forgive oneself is actually due to an anxiety problem. Feeling anxious and unworthy, even when we know we are doing our best, can damage our relationships. At moments like these we are in essence rejecting God's mercy, a priceless divine gift that is always available to us.

Someone who continually looks for the good in themselves and in their spouse will strengthen their marriage by being merciful regarding any shortcomings in either. When someone deserts a spouse and family, the one who remains can avoid anger and revenge and look upon the former spouse with mercy. Mercy is always the most powerful guiding principle in a relationship, even a relationship that has been injured or broken. This does not mean that one should ignore the importance of sin, but it does mean that one should remember the infinite power of Christ's Atonement.

Living in mercy—living *with* mercy—frees us from the rigidity of harsh judgments that can lead to misery, allowing us to feel the same kind of mercy for others that God feels for them and for us. This goes beyond saying, "I'm sorry," or "I forgive you." It's deeper—a strongly held inner conviction that moves us to love others, even those who may have deeply hurt us. If we *love* mercy, as Elder Dale G. Renlund has taught, we will begin to *live* in mercy.[2] Mercy will grow inside us. We will naturally be drawn to receive power from God to move forward, no matter

---

2. Dale G. Renlund, "Do Justly, Love Mercy, and Walk Humbly With God," *Ensign*, November 2020.

how difficult the road may seem, and to be merciful toward ourselves and to others. His enabling power, His grace, will sustain us in the darkest of hours when hope seems impossible.

Living in mercy helps us look past mistakes, and living in grace gives us the power to move forward, pick up the pieces, redirect our thoughts and actions, and become a new creature. This is the power of God's mercy and the power of His grace, a power that springs from compassion. These two gifts from God can change us if we let them. And when we let them change us, our attachment to God and to others can be transformed. In some cases we may need to seek professional therapy to help undo the wrongs of the past, but seeking therapy is simply one way to access God's grace, like seeking orthopedic surgery when we tear an ACL. The Redeemer's power can heal us in many ways. If we have been abused, ignored, neglected, or forgotten by anyone in our current circle of love, we can be healed by living in mercy and in grace. When we seek these God-given blessings, they live in us.

In moments of severe trial or painful remembering we no longer wonder if God has forgotten us, and we no longer feel hopeless at improving our attachment to God and to others. All can be changed. We can feel closer to God, feel His power, and see a new future unfold, a future filled with His love.

Invitations:

Open yourself to mercy.
Let it live inside you.
Forgive yourself, even when it seems impossible.
Welcome God's grace.
Let it live inside you.
Forget the mistakes and move forward.

CARE FOR THE
WHOLE SOUL

*Come unto Him, and offer your whole souls
as an offering unto Him.*

—Omni 1:26

We tend to think that our emotional problems originate in the brain. But the body is so tightly linked with the spirit that we cannot treat each separately. More important, most emotional problems emerge because of relational conflicts. There's no question that when Lehi was berated by a family member, the conflict caused both physical and emotional pain. The quality of our attachments with one another affects our whole soul—body as well as spirit. One psychologist has said, "Our attachment needs are so salient that they can be measured physiologically. For example, if you have a safe, loving, relationship, your heart rate decreases, you have fewer stress hormones, and your body works more efficiently."[1] Logically the reverse is true also: If we want to strengthen our attachments, we need to focus on our physical, emotional, and spiritual health. Both the body and the spirit lead

---

1. Jason N Linder, "The Psycho-Physiology of Relationships: What You Don't Know," *Psychology Today,* July 12, 2020, https://www.psychologytoday.com/us/blog/relationship-and-trauma-insights/202007/the-psycho-physiology-relationships-what-you-dont-know

to our overall attachment or relational health, our ability to give and receive love effectively.

When President Russell M. Nelson was sustained as President and Prophet of The Church of Jesus Christ of Latter-day Saints, a news commentator marveled at how healthy the newly sustained leader was considering his age. The co-anchor agreed and said in essence, "Well, he's a heart doctor, so he knows what to eat and how to take care of himself." The comment caused me to chuckle. Everyone who is aware of President Nelson is impressed by his physical health given his age, and most know that he practiced medicine prior to his call as a member of the Twelve. But do we really think that it is simply his knowledge about caring for his body that causes him to enjoy such good health in his nineties? Many have the knowledge, but only a few act on that knowledge. Knowing and doing are not the same.

Three-fourths of Americans say that physical exercise is essential to good health, but only one in five actually meets the minimum exercise guidelines, according the US Centers for Disease Control and Prevention.[2] That's exercise. What about diet? We're not doing any better with our eating than we are with our physical activity. When a national study was conducted to assess how Americans view diet and health, most said that Americans are paying more attention to eating healthy foods, but most people also said that Americans are less healthy.[3] In others words, everyone knows we are generally eating too much total food and eating too little of the right foods, but that has not led to a change in actual eating behavior. In short, President Nelson's knowledge

---

2. Amy Norton, "Study: Americans want to be fit, but don't put in the work," *UPI Health News*, June 20, 2017, https://www.upi.com/Health_News/2017/06/20/Study-Americans-want-to-be-fit-but-dont-put-in-the-work/2821497970498/

3. Pew Research Center, "The New Food Fights: U.S. Public Divides Over Food Science," *Science and Society*, December 1, 2016, https://www.pewresearch.org/science/2016/12/01/public-views-about-americans-eating-habits/

about how to care for the body apparently affects his behavior more than it does for most of the rest of us.

Nearly 80 percent of all smokers wish they could quit.[4] A large national study also showed that during the past ten years more people are trying to lose weight to become healthier, but Americans' average weight has actually increased.[5] Trends like these are common. People know they should exercise more, but they don't. They know they should cut back on their sugar intake, but they keep eating more sugar.[6] Knowledge does not necessarily lead to appropriate action.

The Apostle Paul lamented that his actions did not always match up with his intentions: "For what I would, that do I not; but what I hate, that do I" (Romans 7:20). Thus he was asking himself, "Why do I do what I don't really want to do, and fail to do what I know I should do?" So, the news commentator who was amazed at President Nelson's good health may have exclaimed, "How is it that he actually does what he knows he should do?"

While I was seated at a dinner table next to President and Sister Nelson, I began talking about physical health, and Sister Nelson reminded me that President Nelson went skiing every Monday in the winter. As I remember the conversation, she continued with a smile on her face, "He came home after his ski trip last week and said, 'I think skiing every Monday makes me a better husband.' Then I said, 'In that case, you can go skiing every day!'" Sister Nelson was, of course, joking with us, but in some ways their conversation was profound. Exercise does

4. Lydia Saad, "Most Smokres Wish They Could Quit," Gallup News Service, 2002, https://news.gallup.com/poll/7270/most-smokers-wish-they-could-quit.aspx.
5. Ann Sandolu, "Average US BMI on the rise despite increasing weight loss efforts," *Medical News Today,* November 1, 2019, https://www.medical-newstoday.com/articles/327053.
6. "U.S. adult consumption of added sugars increased by more than 30% over three decades," *Science Daily*, November 4, 2014, https://www.sciencedaily.com/releases/2014/11/141104141731.htm.

more than improve physical health; it also affects our emotional health. Those who exercise regularly commonly note that doing so gives them a feeling of well-being, and someone who has a feeling of well-being is more likely to have a positive outlook, an uplifting mood—all of which helps an individual be a better spouse or friend.

After reviewing the research on the effects of exercise on emotional health, a Harvard psychiatrist convincingly described how his first prescription for those suffering from depression and anxiety is not a drug but regular physical exercise: "I want to cement the idea that exercise has profound impact on cognitive abilities and mental health. It is simply one of the best treatments we have for most psychiatric problems."[7] The link between exercise and mental health is clear, but there is also an increasing body of research showing that what we eat affects not only our body but our mind as well.[8] Eating right, exercising regularly, and learning to handle stress have dramatic effects on our emotional and spiritual well-being.

The healthier we are physically, emotionally, and spiritually, the greater will be our capacity to form lasting, healthy attachments. Consider, for example, how our overall health impacts those around us: our families, co-workers, and friends. If we are experiencing any type of mental disorder, physical illness, or spiritual decline, our ability to begin or continue a healthy relationship is significantly compromised.

The Restoration has helped us understand that as children of God our soul consists of both a body and a spirit. Stated simply by the Lord, "And the spirit and the body are the soul of man" (D&C 88:15). Only at death is the body completely separated

7. John J. Ratey and Eric Hagerman, *Spark: The Revolutionary New Science of Exercise and the Brain* (New York: Little, Brown Spark, 2008).
8. Eva Selhub, "Nutritional psychiatry: Your brain on food," *Harvard Health Publishing*, November 16, 2015, https://www.health.harvard.edu/blog/nutritional-psychiatry-your-brain-on-food-201511168626.

from the spirit. Focusing exclusively on physical health or on mental health will never yield the benefits that a dual focus can yield. Thus, if we want to develop healthy, lasting attachments with God and with others, we need to stay mentally, physically, and spiritually healthy. We need to remember that our body and spirit are both priceless gifts from God and that we must care for our whole soul by eating well, exercising, getting adequate sleep, handling the stress in our lives, listening to spiritual promptings, treasuring up the word of God, and praying for divine assistance.

President Nelson has not only set an example for the members of the Church regarding our health, but he has also clearly taught that physical and spiritual health must be considered together. He said: "We will be careful about which counsel we heed. Many so-called experts give advice for the body—without thought for the spirit. Anyone who accepts direction contrary to the Word of Wisdom, for example, forsakes a law revealed to bring both physical and spiritual blessings."[9]

The oneness of spirit and body that comprises our soul is a key to forming healthy attachments. When we do anything that has the potential to improve our physical health, our mental-spiritual health can improve as well. And when we do something to address our mental-spiritual condition, we will feel better physically. Gratitude is a spiritual quality. When we reflect on our blessings, we recognize, draw closer to God, and strengthen our attachment to Him. When we feel gratitude for our spouse or friend, we experience the same benefit. Feeling grateful improves our relationships; it also reduces blood pressure, decreases our risk of chronic disease, and helps us avoid feelings of depression and anxiety.

Caring for the whole soul is one of the most powerful ways to be filled with the Lord's love. God becomes a part of our caring process. Thinking of the love that He has for us and expressing

---

9.   Russell M. Nelson, "We Are Children of God," *Ensign*, November 1998.

that love to others brings newness of spirit, more trust, more confidence, more closeness. But caring for one's soul is not a do-it-yourself project. We need to help one another. Why do most people fail at weight control or at diet or exercise goals? They simply don't have enough support from those close to them. Caring for the whole soul is communal. A spouse, a friend, or a coach can help us fulfill our intentions. Counting the days that we succeed at some new positive habit can help. Sharing our progress with others can help. Recognizing that the Lord will help us care for our whole soul will help.

Whatever approach we use, we keep remembering that this miraculous body the Lord has given us is literally the home for the spirit that God Himself birthed. He is our Eternal Father. He will not forsake us in our efforts to find peace with our body in this mortal state. He will help us find the unity of our body and spirit. He will inspire us, lift us, and guide us, and because we are His—wholly His—we will succeed.

Invitations:

> *Recognize how your body affects your spirit,*
> *and how your spirit affects your body.*
> *Care daily for both body and spirit.*
> *Renew your physical and spiritual energy*
> *so you can lift others.*
> *Learn what it means to offer your whole soul.*

TASTE TRUTH

Truth is truth. The arbiter of truth is God.[1]
—Russell M. Nelson

Mao Zedong, the Chinese leader who brought communism to his people in 1949, had a favorite saying that endured beyond his rule: "Seek truth from facts."[2] That four-word sentence encapsulated his view of truth and influenced the view of many others: if you cannot see it, hear it, feel it, touch it, or smell it, it does not exist. Those few words supported Mao's belief that God did not exist and led the majority of his fellow citizens to atheism.

The Chinese graduate student I mentioned earlier developed a special affection for the restored Church of Jesus Christ while she was pursuing her studies. Although she was never baptized, she regularly attended church meetings and contributed in any way she could. One day she exclaimed, "I wish I could believe in God. I've tried, but I just can't. I was taught since my childhood that the 'facts' were all that mattered, and that if you can't see something, it doesn't exist." Somewhere inside she seemed to feel that God might exist because she heard so many bear testimony

---

1. Russell M. Nelson, "The Love and Laws of God," Brigham Young University devotional, September 17, 2019, https://speeches.byu.edu/talks/russell-m-nelson/love-laws-god/
2. "Seek truth from facts," Wikipedia, 2020, https://en.wikipedia.org/wiki/Seek_truth_from_facts.

of His reality. But she was never able to come to a knowledge of that truth herself.

Most would agree that facts alone do not constitute truth. We ask, "Whose facts? What was the background of the person who stated the facts? What if facts conflict—which facts do I accept as truth?" Facts are simply pieces of information gathered, analyzed, and presented by people who have their own beliefs and feelings that might influence the facts. Facts do not exist independent of the person who is stating them or reading about them. Truth must be embodied. The interchange between Jesus and His disciples is crucial to our understanding of truth. Thomas asked Jesus to show him some facts—the "way" they should go. Jesus responded: "I am the way, the truth, and the life: no man cometh unto the Father, but by me" (John 14:6). Then Philip asked if Jesus could show them the Father, and Jesus replied, "Have I been so long time with you, and yet hast thou not known me, Philip? He that hath seen me hath seen the Father; and how sayest thou then, Shew us the Father?" (John 14:9)

Jesus was trying to help His disciples understand that truth is truth, that it is embodied in both Him and in the Father, so when one has come to know the Son—the embodiment of all truth— one has come to know the Father, who is also the embodiment of all truth. The disciples wanted facts, more information, but what they were seeking was standing right in front of them—the Son of God. And what was essential was not to learn more facts; what was needed was to come to know Jesus, that He was who He said He was, that His Father and He were one—that They were the "way, the truth, and the life."

The implications for everyone who professes a belief in the Savior of the World and in His Eternal Father are clear: The closer we come to Them, the more we will understand all the truth we may need at a given time to help us live so that we can return to Their presence. The point is not for disciples to be able to describe the height and weight or the hair and eye color of Jesus; the point is to come to know Him as their personal Redeemer, the One who is full of mercy, grace, and truth.

In the King Follett discourse the Prophet Joseph taught that good doctrine was not only true but that one could taste it, and the taste was sweet: "This is good doctrine. It tastes good. I can taste the principles of eternal life, and so can you. They are given to me by the revelations of Jesus Christ; and I know that when I tell you these words of eternal life as they are given to me, you taste them, and I know that you believe them. You say honey is sweet, and so do I. I can also taste the spirit of eternal life. I know it is good; and when I tell you of these things which are given me by inspiration of the Holy Spirit, you are bound to receive them as sweet, and rejoice more and more."[3]

The Prophet, of course, was not implying that we taste truth with our tongue's taste buds, but that we taste it with our spiritual sense of taste. I believe he was also saying more. He was helping us understand that any time we hear a truth, we need to experience it, and the only way to thoroughly understand any doctrine or principle is to live it. If someone wants to know if the Word of Wisdom or the law of tithing is true, they need to live the principle and "taste" its effects in their life. The sweetness of that taste comes to them because the living of the doctrine brings them closer to the one who embodies the truth. This is how one draws closer to the Lord. And when we draw closer to the Lord, He draws closer to us. Not only do we learn more about the power of the principle we're living, but we also strengthen our attachment to God.

Elder Neal A. Maxwell taught that agency is key to developing our taste for truth: "We are also to use our agency so that we come to prefer, and even strongly desire, the taste of gospel goodness, sweetness, and joy. Only those who have significantly

---

3.   Joseph Smith, Jr., "The King Follett Sermon," *Documentary History of the Church* 6:302–17, April 7, 1884.

developed the taste buds of the soul will be even partially prepared for the incredible beauties of the world ahead."[4]

I want the sweet taste of truth to flow through me more and more. I want to come to know the giver of truth more and more. Nothing in mortality can match it. Nothing can bring us more happiness than feeling close to the Savior and His Father. Nothing. The reason relationships are the driving force of our existence is that every time we draw closer to God, we simultaneously draw closer to others. Love begets love. So when we distance ourselves from truth, which is also distancing ourselves from God, we weaken, damage, or injure the attachments we have with others. When we seek truth and live it, it becomes embodied in us; it becomes ours, and no one can take it away from us. That process of seeking and living truth by tasting it every day will help us come to know the Lord and others in truth. We will come to know who they really are. When that happens, we are filled with His love.

Remember that the Father and the Son embody all truth.

Invitations:

Taste the sweetness of each gospel truth as it comes to you.
Learn to embody truth by living it.
Let truth draw you closer to God.

---

4.   Neal A. Maxwell, 1999. *One More Strain of Praise* (Salt Lake City, Utah: Deseret Book, 1999), 84–85.

EMBRACE THE UNEXPECTED

Often our opportunities to show
our love come unexpectedly.[1]

—Thomas S. Monson

While teaching a missionary preparation course, I asked students to keep track of how many people they met for the first time. Just saying "hi" to someone was not enough. They needed to have a real conversation with each new person they met. I explained that on their missions, all day every day, they would be meeting people for the first time, and they needed to practice this skill prior to the mission field if they wanted to be prepared. This assignment did not count toward their grade, but students invested themselves in it with real energy and commitment. Each week they would text or e-mail me their results for the week.

One week a student reported having conversations with seventy-two people he had never met before. That's impressive. I asked him in class, "How did you do that in one week? How did you visit with so many?" He responded, "Oh, I was standing in lines a lot this past week, and so I would just ask the person next to me to hold my place in the line, and then I would move

---

1.   Thomas S. Monson, "Love—The Essence of the Gospel," *Ensign*, May 2014.

through the line and introduce myself and talk to as many people as I could." Then he concluded with a profound comment: "You know, Brother Osguthorpe, the surprising thing is that I really think I made some friends I will have the rest of my life."

This student could have avoided the assignment all together, or he could have fulfilled it with minimal effort. But he went beyond what I expected, and because he did that, he experienced something far beyond what he anticipated. Rather than ignoring the unexpected blessings of his actions, he embraced them. He made friends he never expected to make. He connected with some of those seventy-two new acquaintances and subsequently spent time with them—time that he never would have spent had he not been willing to embrace the unexpected.

Life throws us curve balls almost every day. We plan to do something, but then someone calls and our plans change. We set a goal and then see that we need to change it. The things we call interruptions are the unexpected events that cause us to change our original plans. In my first administrative role, I felt frustrated most of the first year in the position. Just when I began to accomplish what I saw as an essential task, someone would knock on my door, wanting to talk with me. They were usually faculty or students who had a problem they did not feel they could solve on their own, so they came for help. Sometimes the problem was serious and complicated. Other times it was something that could be solved in a few minutes. But whatever the size of the problem, it interrupted my thought, diverted me from my original task, and frustrated me.

Somewhere in the second year of my assignment, I began to see things more clearly. The people coming to my door were not keeping me from doing my job. They *were* my job. That's why I had been asked to sit in that administrative seat—to help members of the organization solve their problems. It was the unexpected nature of what I originally saw as intrusions that was so challenging for me. Once I shifted my focus—once I could see that my visitors were not interruptions or intrusions—I could welcome them whenever they came, whatever they wanted. I learned to leave my door open. I was learning to embrace the unexpected—not only to tolerate their visits but to embrace them.

In our marriage relationships, our friendships, and even our relationships with God, we need to embrace the unexpected if we want to strengthen our attachments. As I think back on that first year as an administrator, I worry about how some people may have felt who came to my office. I never turned people away, but at times they probably sensed that I wanted to turn them away. I experienced a steep learning curve, and if a visitor got caught somewhere on that curve, they probably went away from the visit with little new insight. More important, I wonder what effects my internal struggles had on the relationship with the person who came for help. I am quite certain that the relationship was not strengthened.

The scriptures are full of examples of people who embraced the unexpected. Pahoran did not expect Moroni to write such a scathing letter. Moroni's complaints could have offended him, but they didn't. The Samaritan could have passed by the wounded man on his way to Jericho, as the priest and Levite had done, but he stopped and helped the man. He did not expect to find the man lying almost dead on the road, but rather than pass by, he literally embraced the unexpected. No one expected that Cornelius would seek after Christianity, and no one expected that Peter would visit him, a Gentile, and baptize him. But both of them embraced the unexpected, and their openness changed both of them and led to a remarkable increase in the spread of the gospel.

When someone close to us says or does something unexpected, can we welcome the surprise and seek to understand the person? When a child makes a mistake or wants to do something against the parents' wishes, can the parent embrace the unexpected rather than shutting the child out? When a spouse changes his or her mind and wants to go the direction opposite from the original plan, can the other spouse patiently seek to find out what underlies the change? Can they talk until understanding comes? Can they embrace each other in the midst of the misunderstanding? Those with an avoidant or anxious attachment style have difficulty embracing the unexpected. The avoidant person may not feel the need to help anyone else. The anxious individual may lack confidence to give the assistance desired by another. Only those with a secure, enduring attachment with God can embrace the unexpected with ease.

Job did not expect to suffer as he did. He did not expect to lose everything and everyone precious around him, but he held on in spite of the unexpected and embraced God even in his darkest moments. When the brother of Jared asked God to help him provide light in the barges, he was likely expecting God to solve the problem for him, but God did the unexpected. He asked the brother of Jared to come up with the solution himself and present it. The brother of Jared embraced that unexpected moment and took a solution to the Lord. If Job had distanced himself from God in his unexpected suffering, or if the brother of Jared had refused to work out and propose his solution for the dark barges, their relationship with God would have been damaged. So it is with us. Welcoming the difficult moment that we did not anticipate, reaching out and embracing something we had not sought, can bring us closer to God and to each other. It can fill us with his love.

Invitations:

> *Be flexible.*
> *Don't let plans get in your way.*
> *Welcome the one who needs you.*
> *Embrace the unexpected.*

PRAY ALWAYS

*If ye will repent and harden not your hearts,
immediately shall the great plan of redemption
be brought about unto you.*

—Alma 34:31

Prayer is the lifeline that links us to the Lord. When we listen and learn from the Spirit, we strengthen that lifeline, and our attachment to God becomes preeminent in our lives. Nothing else is as important. Nothing can come between us. Nothing can break the link. We are open, ready, and eager to heed His prompting and follow wherever it leads.

President Russell M. Nelson has urged us to "Hear Him," just as God the Father urged Joseph when the young prophet-to-be knelt in that grove of trees on that transcendent spring day.[1] Like Joseph, we must strive to be open, ready, and eager for the Lord's message for us. If not, we may not hear Him. It is as if we are surrounded every hour of every day with divine messages, messages that the Lord wants us to receive, but the messages often go unnoticed or ignored because we are not open, ready, and eager to listen, heed, and follow.

The real question is, how can we remain open, ready, and eager to receive the voice of the Lord in our lives? Young Joseph

---

1.   Russell M. Nelson, "Hear Him," *Ensign*, May 2020.

was so open, so ready, and so eager. Perplexity preceded his prayer. In his case, it was perplexity with the conflicting religious messages of his day. Perplexity often precedes our most meaningful prayers: Should I marry this person? Should we have another child? Should I make a change in my career? Joseph was perplexed by external conflicts in messages he was hearing from various ministers, but then those external conflicts caused internal conflicts in his own heart. He was not sure where to turn. He could not answer his question without divine help.

Internal conflicts are the most difficult to resolve. Two internal forces seem to be struggling against each other, as if our spiritual immune system is turning on itself in the same self-destructive way our physical immune system turns on itself when we contract an autoimmune disease. These diseases typically cannot cure themselves. They can be managed, and many can be prevented, but they cannot be cured. Spiritual autoimmune disorders, however, can be both prevented and cured by yielding ourselves to the Lord and partaking of His mercy and His grace.

The Book of Mormon teaches that when we soften our heart by giving up a negative thought, act, or event—even if that thought, act, or event seems small and insignificant—we can "immediately" begin to feel the power of the redemption in our lives (Alma 34:31). We do not need to correct every weakness we have ever had in our lives in order to feel the Lord's presence. We need only to open ourselves to His mercy by forgiving ourself for some mistake, or by forgiving someone else who has wronged us. The very minute we become merciful, the Lord's mercy floods in, and we are changed.

Nothing can strengthen our attachment to God more than the simple softening of our heart. If our heart is hard, we become rigid, unforgiving of ourselves and others, and we close ourselves off to the Spirit. But when we become open, ready, and eager to improve—to draw closer to Him—He immediately draws closer to us. We do not need to wait for Him, but He is willing to wait for us for however long it takes. Our attachment to God is thus uneven. Our love for Him can never rise to the level of His love for us. His love is infinite, ours is developing. We may be momentarily unprepared to accept His love, but He is never unprepared to give His love to us. We are His total reason for being.

When we pray always, we strive never to close ourselves off to the Spirit. When we observe outward conflicts that trouble us, or when we experience internal conflicts that bring perplexity, we focus on faith, knowing that the Lord will give us what we need when we need it, if we can only recognize it when it comes.

Is it possible for one person to help another to pray always? Or is prayer so private, so personal that it can be experienced only by oneself? Can a parent help a child learn how to "pray always"? Can spouses help each other learn how to pray always? Can a friend help another friend learn to do this? The thoughts that lift us and draw us closer to what is good and true are prayers of the heart, and when we express these to each other, we are virtually helping another learn what it means to be open, ready, and eager for the Lord's help. Children who know a parent is praying for them learn how to pray always. Spouses who know they are praying for each other learn how to pray always. And friends who know that friends are praying for them also learn.

It is common for someone to say, "I've been praying for you." Then the other person responds, "Yes, I have felt your prayers." Such prayers can be uttered formally or unexpressed in mental pleadings. Either way, the one being prayed for and the one doing the praying are both learning about what it means to pray always—to be open, ready, and eager for divine connection. Our physical distance from God shrinks when we have prayers in our heart throughout the day. Even though He is not physically close, He does not leave us "comfortless." The Spirit can always be close when we draw close to the Lord in our thoughts and prayers.

Invitations:

> *Pray always.*
> *Be open, ready, and eager.*
> *Keep strengthening your attachment to God.*

GROW IN HOLINESS

Whatever our personal circumstance,
wherever we may be on the covenant path home,
may our prayers for greater holiness be answered.[1]

—Henry B. Eyring

I pause before entering the temple and gaze at the inscription above the door: "Holiness to the Lord, The House of the Lord." I have always understood the second phrase, The House of the Lord, but I begin to wonder more about the meaning of the first phrase. It does not say, Holiness *of* the Lord; it is apparently not referring to the Lord's holiness. It must be referring to *my* holiness—the one who is entering the temple. It might say, "Bring all the holiness that you can into the Lord's house." Then I pause again. But holiness means spiritual perfection, and I know that's impossible in this life, as President Russell M. Nelson has taught throughout his ministry.[2] My mortality overcomes me for a minute. What holiness can I possibly bring into the Lord's house with all of my imperfections?

Holiness connotes spiritual purity; it means I should become more like my Heavenly Father and His Son, Jesus Christ. This

---

1. Henry B. Eyring, "Holiness and the Plan of Happiness," *Ensign*, November 2019.
2. Russell M. Nelson, *Perfection Pending: And Other Favorite Discourses* (Salt Lake City, Utah: Deseret Book Company, 1998).

still seems impossible, though I recognize that complete perfection is not achieved in this life. Even a little perfection seems beyond my reach. And yet, here I am waiting to enter the temple, a place where I feel the Lord's holiness, a place where I can feel His perfect love, a place where I come so that I can feel closer to Him and even learn to be more like Him.

Before I enter the temple, I sit for a moment on a nearby bench and reflect on the the Savior. I see Him kneeling in prayer, praying not only for His disciples but for all who would believe their words and come unto Him. And I recall His plea to the Father—that His disciples would be one as He and His Father are one. Because of the Restoration we know that God the Father and His Son are physically separate beings. So, we can interpret His plea for oneness as a plea for spiritual unity, spiritual attachment. He was praying that His disciples would love and support each other so much and so purely that they would be spiritually unified, connected, and attached.

In this prayer the Lord prayed not only for His live present disciples, but also for all of us who would yet be born—everyone who would believe and draw close to Him: "That they all may be one; as thou, Father, art in me, and I in thee, that they also may be one in us" (John 17:21). This oneness is a quality of holiness. He might have prayed, "Bless my disciples that they can learn to be holy as thou Father art holy and as I am holy. Bless them to learn to be like us." He gave us commandments, covenants, and ordinances to help us achieve this quality of holiness. The sacrament is a powerful example. We figuratively put Christ in us as we partake of the sacrament so that He can be in us and we can be in Him, so that our attachment to Him can be strengthened. Those with an anxious attachment style may worry that such oneness with God can never be accomplished, while those with an avoidant style may purposefully stay distant from God so they are not disappointed.

The healthier and more secure our attachment style is, the more we will seek oneness with God. As Elder D. Todd Christofferson has taught, "If we yearn to dwell in Christ and have Him dwell in us, then holiness is what we seek, in both body and spirit. We seek it in the temple, whereon is inscribed 'Holiness to the Lord.' We seek it in our marriages, families, and homes. We seek it each week as we delight in the Lord's holy day. We seek it even in the details of daily living: our speech, our dress, our thoughts."[3]

Elder Christofferson was teaching that holiness is the key to strengthening our relationship with God—holiness in both body and spirit. We need to care for the whole soul. Our physical body or our spirit will never be perfect in this life, but it is the act of seeking such purity and holiness that we may become closer to God, so that He can come closer to us. If we do not understand something about how He sees us, how He loves us, and how He trusts us, then we cannot learn to see Him, love Him, and trust Him to give us the strength to become like Him.

My pondering on the bench finally ends, and I clasp the door handle on the large entry door and approach the recommend desk. Once inside the chapel before beginning the ordinance, I seem to see nothing but light streaming through the stained glass windows:

Light

Light flooding in,
washing away the darkness
and the ugliness of the world.

Light flooding in,
opening my mind.
Showing me for the first time
who I am, and the person I can become.

Light flooding in
again and again and again.
Never stopping, never slowing down.

---

3.   D. Todd Christofferson, "The Living Bread Which Came Down From Heaven," *Ensign*, November 2017.

Light and more light
until I see and sense and know
He has not forgotten me.

He has not left me alone
in the shadows to stumble and fall.
Deep inside I feel the light.

More deeply still I understand.
I am changed by Him
and will never be the same
again.

Still seated in the room with light flooding in, I pray silently with all the spiritual energy I possess that I can be filled with His love. I yearn to feel more intensely His love for me so that I can show that love more graciously, more freely to others. Only then can holiness increase in me. Only then can my own view gradually become more clear so that one day I will see Him as He is. And finally I pray that those I love, some who are living with me, as well as others who have gone before or are yet to be born, might also grow in holiness so that one day when the Savior returns we will see each other—parents and children, eternal companions, siblings, and friends. At that singular moment of holy attachment, we will embrace, hold each other in our arms, never to be separated again, always to be one.

Invitations:

Seek holiness.
Know that the Lord can sanctify you.
Seek for light.
Be filled with His love.
Pray for others to be filled also.
Treasure every moment in His holy house.

SAFE, SECURE, AND ENDURING

Dwelling in safety, security, and enduring joy forever.

In part one I discussed the meaning of attachment to others, the importance of parent-child attachment, and how the quality of relationships early in life can affect the quality of adult relationships, particularly marriage. In part two I focused on the attachment that one forms with God, how that attachment affects our relationships with others, and how human and divine attachments affect each other. In part three I suggested ways to strengthen our attachment with God and with others.

On the way to this lifelong goal, most encounter at least to some degree anxiety, avoidance, or both as they form relationships. The chart on the following page shows how either of these negative approaches can lead to unhealthy attachments:

Anxiety and avoidance are the twin enemies of forming healthy attachments in mortality. Those who allow anxiety to rule in their relationships feel unsafe because they are in constant fear that their love will not be reciprocated, that their desire for wholeness will crumble. That fear paradoxically can lead to a deep sense of insecurity, the very outcome they most wish to avoid. And until that fear is gradually replaced with faith in the Lord Jesus Christ and in the one they love, their relationship will be in jeopardy.

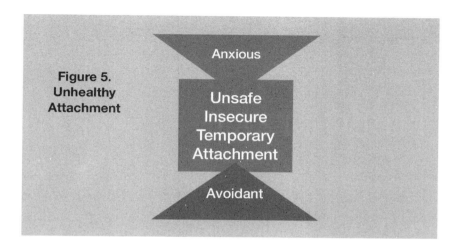

Figure 5. Unhealthy Attachment

Anxious

Unsafe
Insecure
Temporary
Attachment

Avoidant

Like relational anxiety, relational avoidance can literally prohibit someone from forming a healthy, lasting attachment, because avoidant individuals will simply not allow themselves to get close to others. Those who distance themselves from others or from God eventually find themselves in temporary relationships that leave them feeling empty and alone, longing for something they see as unreachable, and losing purpose and meaning in their life. No matter how competent they might be, how self-assured in their own ability to go it alone, most of them ultimately discover that joy does not come in isolation.

The good news is that anxious and avoidant feelings can be overcome, particularly as one comes to rely on the mercy and grace of the Savior's Atonement. Anxiety can be changed into feelings of security. Avoidance can be replaced by enduring love for God and for others. This is the intent of part three: to help us overcome the unproductive, ineffective patterns we may have developed that can lead to unhappiness with our spouse, a family member, a friend, or God. When the suggestions offered in part three are put into practice, I am convinced that attachments can be strengthened. The more we practice these relational principles, the healthier our attachments will become. As shown in the following chart, feelings of avoidance or anxiety can fade away

171

when we open ourselves and permit the Lord to change our hearts through his mercy and grace:

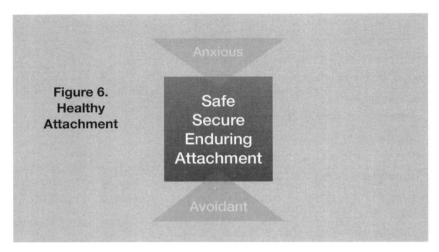

Figure 6. Healthy Attachment

Most of us have experienced feelings of relational avoidance or anxiety at some point in life. Even though these feelings may not have prohibited us from forming lasting attachments, they may still diminish the quality of our relationship in some way. No attachment is static. Relationships are fluid and alive. They need to be nurtured and protected like all living things. Otherwise they can wither and even die. God's covenant children by definition have committed themselves to form safe, secure, enduring attachments. He gave us commandments, covenants, temples, scriptures, and living prophets to help us achieve this very aim. He knew that success would come only with our commitment, love, faith, and action. The Savior knew that exaltation is a family matter, that no one could be exalted alone. That is precisely why He came to earth, lived among mere mortals, and demonstrated by His teachings and His life how essential it is to be filled with His love.

EPILOGUE: LET LOVE CHANGE YOU

When he shall appear we shall be like him,
for we shall see him as he is;
that we may have this hope;
that we may be purified even as he is pure.

—Moroni 7:48

I began this book by describing my search for answers to questions about the relationships we form with God and with others. I first described an experience I had in my youth with Shawn, a friend who had decided to leave his family and the Church. I continued by describing some of the questions that arose as I pursued relationships with missionary companions and later with my wife and children. To understand the full meaning and power of love in all relationships I recounted the story of Amanda, one who never knew parental love. Her story brings into graphic clarity how essential love is for our growth and development, and yes, our very survival. Amanda eventually found parental love and was sealed to her adoptive parents. Without their courageous act, no one knows what might have happened to that forlorn little girl.

There is no question that love deprivation changes human beings in dramatically disastrous ways. Those who feel unloved, unwanted, or forgotten struggle through life because they lack the capacity to form lasting healthy attachments with God and with others. Because they do not experience real love, they have difficulty giving it to others. The COVID-19 pandemic has helped illuminate the problem. Not only has the virus caused physical illness and death, but it has also inflicted an unprecedented scourge of loneliness on so many. One writer has called loneliness the "shadow pandemic."[1] Loneliness has no preference for age, gender, or race. It can attack anyone. And *loneliness* is simply a term we use to describe a person who feels unloved, unwanted, or forgotten.

Recognizing the negative effects of parental rejection, abuse, or neglect, the pain of marital discord, or the dark results of a pandemic can help us see the "brightness of hope" the gospel brings to those who embrace it. The adoptive family members who welcomed Amanda into their home changed her. She no longer had to feel forgotten. Similarly, Malu, the young thirteen-year-old girl who was separated from her mother during wartime in Africa, highlights the power of extended family members to step in when parents cannot be present. The love of adoptive parents changed Amanda. The love of an uncle and other extended family members changed Malu.

This is the central message of this book: that by increasing our capacity to give and receive love, we will be changed. We will become more like the Savior and one day live with Him and His Father again.

My wife's love has changed me in countless positive ways. She teaches me something every day about loving others and loving God. She reaches out to others, whether or not such reaching is convenient. Her capacity to give and receive love amazes me. My children have also changed me, particularly

---

1. Melody M. Warnick, "Behind the headlines of COVID-19 is another far-reaching health crisis," *BYU Magazine,* Summer 2020, https://magazine.byu.edu/article/loneliness-the-shadow-pandemic/

because they are living their lives in such inspiring ways. My siblings have changed me. My Grandma Bessie and her father changed me. My ancestors, such as Lester Russell, have changed me. My friends have changed me, just as my father's friendship with Skip changed both of them. Love changes us. But for the change to occur, we need to accept the love that comes to us from God and from others, and then seek to share that love with as many as possible.

The Lord has said that all we need to do is come and "partake of the waters of life freely" (D&C 10:66). Think of it—the Savior is pouring out His love, His waters of life, to all who will come and partake. But to partake, we must first choose to receive Him. This is precisely how we can make changes, however small or large they might be, in our own attachment style. But we first need to *want* to change. Desire is essential. Only then can we begin to relate to others in healthier ways. When we choose to change, our capacity to give love to others increases. It is not a one-way stream. Love always needs to flow in both directions.

The more we feel His love for us, the more we are empowered to share that same love with others. This is when the richness of eternal attachments envelops us. We begin thinking less about our own needs and more about the needs of others, because God gives us the strength to reach out. When we see divinity in others and we feel love flowing from them to us and from us back to them, lasting, healthy, secure attachments are deepened. No more feelings of neglect. No more feelings of loneliness. Only love. The pure, unaffected love that God has for us and that we can have for His children. My hope and my prayer for myself and for anyone seeking greater happiness is to be filled with His love, not only momentarily, but to be filled today more than yesterday, never to let that love fade, but always nourishing it as a growing, life-giving, gift from God.

ABOUT THE AUTHOR

Russell T. Osguthorpe has authored four books and more than seventy articles on religion and education. He has served as a professor and administrator at Brigham Young University and in a variety of Church callings, including Sunday School General President. He has conducted seminars in more than twenty-five countries, and speaks several languages. He and his wife, Lolly, are the parents of five children and live in Provo, Utah.